Marketing with Social Media

A LITA Guide

Edited by

Beth C. Thomsett-Scott

An imprint of the American Library Association

CHICAGO   2014

Printed in the United States of America

18 17 16 15 14   5 4 3 2 1

Extensive effort has gone into ensuring the reliability of the information in this book; however, the publisher makes no warranty, express or implied, with respect to the material contained herein.

ISBNs: 978-1-55570-972-3 (paper); 978-1-55570-986-0 (PDF); 978-1-55570-987-7 (ePub); 978-1-55570-988-4 (Kindle). For more information on digital formats, visit the ALA Store at alastore.ala.org and select eEditions.

Library of Congress Cataloging-in-Publication Data
Marketing with social media : a LITA guide / Beth C. Thomsett-Scott, editor.
    pages   cm
    Includes bibliographical references and index.
    ISBN 978-1-55570-972-3 (alk. paper)
    1. Libraries—Marketing. 2. Online social networks—Library applications. 3. Social media. I. Thomsett-Scott, Beth C., editor of compilation.
    Z716.3.M2955 2014
    302.30285—dc23   2013042963

Book design in Berkeley and Avenir. Cover image © Cienpies Design / Shutterstock.

♾ This paper meets the requirements of ANSI/NISO Z39.48-1992 (Permanence of Paper).

Marketing with Social Media

*I dedicate this second book to my fantastic daughter,
who continually amazes me with her zeal for life and learning.
Additionally, I dedicate this work to my friends, who kept me
going through some tough times this year, especially Patricia,
Kenneth, Jenne, Bob, Staci, Anna, Donna, and Pat.
Peace to all.*

Contents

Contents

Preface

Marketing with Social Media: A LITA Guide draws vital information together into one work. While there are books and articles discussing technologies or marketing or marketing with technology, there are few works that address multiple technologies or look at implementing a technology in a step-by-step manner. This book is designed to save readers time and effort by providing the basic information on setting up popular or cutting-edge marketing technologies. Several technologies have been around for a while but may have fallen out of early favor, yet still are highly useful tools—especially because we have seen a number of technological innovations in recent years. Readers are introduced to the technologies and guided through the steps to implement them. Information on staffing, training, and assessing the services is provided in order to offer a full spectrum of knowledge about successfully marketing with the technologies.

Using the contributed chapter format allows a wider spectrum of technologies to be covered and to include a greater variety of experiences. The first chapter provides an overview of current technologies, with the following chapters focusing on specific technologies. Each chapter provides a bibliography; the first also provides additional reading and resources to follow up on the content in the book and for readers looking for extra information. Readers will benefit from the plethora of images that clearly describe how to access and implement the free technologies included in the book.

On behalf of the contributors, I wish all readers the very best of luck in designing and implementing their marketing system with a new or redesigned technology.

Acknowledgments

As always, I appreciate the University of North Texas and the UNT Libraries for providing me with a position that lets me stretch myself and continue to grow professionally. Thanks to my supervisors past and present, who have allowed me the freedom to explore new technologies and see how they relate to our work. I am indebted to my colleagues at the Discovery Park Library, who support me in my endeavors. And, of course, much love and appreciation to my family and friends for, well, everything.

Libraries and Marketing with Technology

Anita R. Dryden, Briddle Law Library, University of Pennsylvania

NEW TOOLS FOR GOOD OLD-FASHIONED MARKETING

The rapid advancement of technology has been both a boon and a burden to libraries. While we are lucky to have many new tools available which make our work more efficient and effective, we have a reached a point where libraries—even those at academic institutions—are no longer the sole source for information resources. Libraries have come to terms with this fact in many ways and have begun adjusting their services in the face of widespread competition from Google, Amazon, and the rest of the World Wide Web. As a result, libraries have largely embraced marketing as a necessary tool for survival in this new competitive age (Shontz 2004).

One of the reasons marketing has become so important to libraries is the disconnection between our offerings and user knowledge of these offerings (Cronin and O'Brien 2009). How often have librarians heard a user exclaim, "I had no idea the library could do that!"? Marketing is a way to bridge that gap. Kenneway (2007, 92) notes that "it is not enough just to be good at what you do anymore. You also have to be adept at communicating the good and what it means to your customers."

So what types of things can libraries market? Just about anything! Libraries can market services, events happening in the library, collections, staff expertise, and more. Marketing is really about reaching customers—in this case, library users—and creating connections that resonate with them. While technology has encouraged competition, technology can also help libraries meet this competition through new means of marketing.

This introductory chapter provides an overview of marketing with technology, introduces the technologies included in this book, and suggests best practices. It also offers a reading list for those looking for more information on using technology to market libraries.

THE IMPACT OF TECHNOLOGY ON MARKETING

One of the secrets of the marketing industry is that, for most of its history, practitioners had very little idea whether what they did actually worked. When Don Draper has a genius idea on the TV show *Mad Men*, his agency and customers really do not know whether his campaign brought more customers to Utz's Potato Chips. Even if it did, maybe Peggy's idea would have been more effective. Marketers of the past would often use focus groups to determine advertisement effectiveness, but there was no reliable way to quantify the success of a particular marketing effort in objective terms.

Marketing has become much more of a science with the advent of technology. It is now more feasible to measure the return on investment (ROI) of a marketing effort or the value gained as a result of undertaking a particular effort. Romero (2011) notes that for nonprofit organizations, the "investment" piece of ROI is more likely to be measured in time or effort than actual dollars spent, which is an important consideration for the primarily free technologies discussed in this book. Many of these tools offer metrics and analytics to help you evaluate your marketing efforts. Digital marketing efforts can be much more targeted and measurable than ever before, and the use of technology itself can help disprove outdated notions of what libraries are and what they offer (Kenneway 2007).

Technology has also lowered the bar to entry for effective marketing. Until recently, launching an effective marketing campaign required procuring the services of marketing professionals, either in-house or through an agency, and making expensive and risky advertising "buys" of signage, space in publications, and broadcast time. In short, marketing was expensive and difficult. However, new tools have made it possible for any library with the interest and motivation to market itself with little to no cost and much less time investment.

Despite the many new opportunities that technology brings to marketing, it is important not to overlook traditional marketing principles, including consistent branding and an effective visual representation of the library. Maintaining a consistent "voice" or tone in postings on different services will also help bring cohesion to the library's messaging. As a library spreads its presence across multiple tools and platforms, consistent branding and messaging helps reduce confusion and prove the authenticity of accounts. A variety of resources exist to get libraries up to speed on basic marketing principles, including books by Mathews (2009), providing extremely comprehensive instructions for academic libraries, and Alman (2007), especially helpful to those librarians in small libraries.

SELECTING TOOLS FOR MARKETING

There is a wealth of options for libraries looking for technology tools to include in their marketing efforts, from social media platforms to analytic tools—and even your library's website. However, it is extremely unlikely that any library will want or need to use all these tools. Stuart (2010) notes that librarians must necessarily be selective about which sites to use, as the time and effort involved in creating a presence on every available site far outweighs the potential rewards. Choosing which tools will work for a particular library is a combination of knowing the user population, considering how tools will work together or complement one another, and simple trial and error.

Knowing the audience is of utmost importance. Some technologies require equipment that a particular library's users may not have access to. For example, school librarians whose students are not allowed to use their cell phones during the school day may not see good results with QR codes because these require a smartphone to scan in order to use.

Many marketing tools tie into one another quite easily. A good example of this is Pinterest, where you can sign up using an existing Twitter or Facebook account. Even if you create an account from scratch, there are still buttons throughout the system that allow you to share your pins to the aforementioned platforms and other tools.

Despite the fact that libraries are unlikely to use every new tool or social media platform that is developed, it is good practice to go ahead and register an account with any service that seems to be getting significant notice. User names can be taken quickly on a new service and it is important to keep your institution's account names as consistent as possible across all platforms. Many libraries have similar names or use the same acronyms in their publicity. For example, at the University of Houston, we normally abbreviate everything to *UH*, including, of course, the UH Libraries. However, we are far from the only institution in the country, let

3

alone the world, that uses the *UH* abbreviation. If your library's preferred name is already taken on a service, it may require some more serious thought about how to present your organization within that service.

TECHNOLOGIES FOR DISCUSSION

Facebook

Facebook has become an extremely popular outpost for libraries of all types (figs. 1.1 and 1.2). It is a very popular social networking platform, surpassing one billion users in 2012 (Facebook 2012), which makes it extremely likely that a

FIGURE 1.1
Facebook page for Lexington (KY) Public Library

good portion of most library users are already using the service. For this reason, Facebook is an excellent starting point for libraries looking to make a foray into marketing with technology. Facebook content can also be made "public," making it viewable by anyone, although not all features will be available to users who are not logged in to the service.

There has been an evolution in how Facebook has handled the presence of organizations, such as libraries and businesses, over time. When the current "Pages" system was introduced in 2007, libraries had more options for how to present themselves and now can customize the look and feel of their pages, as

FIGURE 1.2
Facebook page for University of Houston Libraries

well as import content and use application programming interfaces (APIs) from other systems.

Facebook can serve as both a passive and an active marketing tool. In an active sense, libraries can post status updates that their followers can see. They can also purchase ads and target these to specific categories of users. Whenever a user "likes" the library on Facebook, this usually shows up in their friends' timelines, thus alerting more users to the presence of the page and potentially drawing more "likes" in a passive manner. Facebook also allows their ubiquitous "like" buttons to be embedded in external websites, allowing users to "like" particular items outside the Facebook system, which are then reflected on their profiles. Libraries can embed these buttons throughout their larger web presence to increase their reach on Facebook and thus allow users to easily share particular books, services, and more.

Alcock (2009) discusses how the University of Wolverhampton in the UK was able to use their Facebook page to share important links, promote information literacy workshops, and embed search boxes for popular electronic resources. She found that the effort involved in setting up and maintaining a page was minimal and that it is an effective outreach tool for their users who were Facebook members. Fredrick (2012) notes that Facebook is extremely useful as an outreach tool for school libraries, but adds that school librarians should be prepared to address concerns from parents and administrators around the age-appropriateness of the platform for students, privacy concerns, and filters that block social media sites on school computers. More information about Facebook is presented in chapter 2.

Wikis

Named after the Hawaiian word for "quick," Wiki software was developed to allow for quick and simple updating of web content. The success of Wikipedia has brought wiki software to popular attention, and the use of wikis has since become widespread. Libraries use wikis for a variety of purposes, including instruction, virtual reference, desk management, and supplementing digital content offerings—types of content that often have multiple authors and require frequent updates (Jackson et al. 2007). Wiki software reduces the difficulty of keeping such content up to date and facilitates participatory projects between libraries and their users, as well as among multiple libraries.

MediaWiki, the open-source wiki software platform that was originally built to support Wikipedia, is one popular platform used by libraries, as noted in chapter 3. Jackson and colleagues (2007) discuss the use of MediaWiki for subject guide pages which promote electronic resources at the Florida State University libraries. The authors chose to use MediaWiki after concluding that using their main library website for this purpose would have required substantive edits to the structure of the website as well as extensive staff training. MediaWiki is a software package that must be installed locally; libraries wishing to use MediaWiki can visit mediawiki .org to download and install the software package. For libraries who do not wish to install such a robust software package, PB Works (pbworks.com) is an excellent web-based option that offers a basic free version, as well as for-pay options that include more robust features.

Videos

Video sharing sites, such as YouTube and Vimeo, allow libraries to easily post and share video content. Certainly libraries can host streaming video content on their own servers; however, placing content within these popular systems allows it to be easily shared and discovered. Libraries can also create playlists of similar videos and access advanced analytics about how these videos are watched and shared. A 2011 Pew Internet & American Life Project report found that 71 percent of adults use one or more video-sharing website (Moore 2011). These numbers are even higher for adults ages 18 to 29 at 92 percent, with nearly half of this age group indicating that they had used a video sharing site "yesterday."

Libraries create and share many types of video content. Colburn and Haines (2012) discuss seven categories of promotional videos on YouTube: General Promotion/Appreciation, Orientation/Tour, Patron-Generated, Promotion of Service/Collection, Event Documentation, News, and Instruction/Tutorial. They also provide case studies of three well-received promotional videos, including a 2007 project at the University of Minnesota Duluth highlighting a student-made video contest winner. Such contests provide an excellent way to get users engaged with your library in a creative way. Little (2010, 71) advises that videos should be "upbeat, informal, and relatively short," and notes that existing archival video collections can provide a base of ready-made content. The University of Maryland Libraries YouTube page (fig. 1.3) shows an array of videos on varying topics that represent the breadth of services offered by the library.

Video creation involves more time and skill than many of the other technologies discussed in this book; however, libraries that have the interest and ability to undertake video promotion can develop deep and meaningful interactions with users. More information about using videos for marketing is available in Chapter 4.

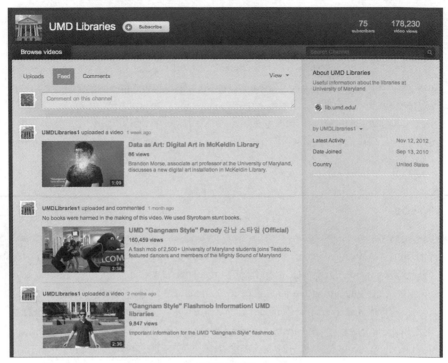

FIGURE 1.3
YouTube page for University of Maryland Library

Pinterest

Pinterest is a social networking platform focused on visual content that allows users to create virtual pinboards of images from across the web, similar to the way that previous generations might have clipped images from magazines to create a scrapbook or a physical bulletin board. Users can create a variety of topical boards, and "pin" images from other places around the web by pasting a short bit of code into their browser's bookmarks bar, as well as by uploading their own images. These images serve as links to the original source of the material. Users can also browse the pinboards of other members that they follow within the service, or popular pins from all users, and are able to repin items onto their own boards. Pinterest differs from other photo-sharing sites, such as Flickr, which are largely intended for sharing individually created content (Thornton 2012).

Pinterest also provides "Pin It!" buttons that can be integrated into external websites to allow users to pin directly from the site without having a bookmark.

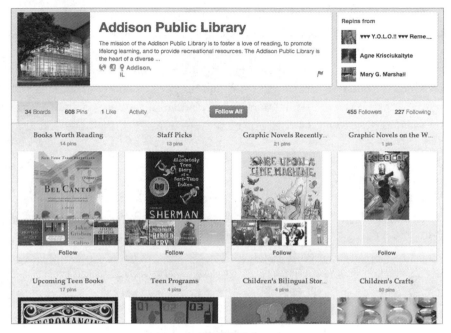

FIGURE 1.4
Pinterest page for Addison (IL) Public Library

Libraries wishing to create a strong presence in Pinterest could consider implementing these buttons within their catalog or discovery system.

When it first began to grow in popularity, Pinterest was often derided as being "just for women," filled with nothing more than pictures of craft projects, wedding dresses, and the actor Ryan Gosling (Thornton 2012). However, as the system has grown, its value as a tool for sharing visual information has spread to all types of users, and the system has largely lost this stigma. In fact, reports show that Pinterest is extremely successful at driving traffic to retailers, and as a result, many retailers have begun to encourage use of the service (Thornton 2012).

Pinterest has already reached a wide following among educators who use it to curate ideas for their classrooms (Falk 2012). Libraries could use Pinterest to share cover art of new book acquisitions, children's craft programs, or ideas for redesigns of library spaces. The Addison (IL) Public Library's Pinterest page demonstrates several types of boards that libraries can create (fig. 1.4). A nice functionality of the system is that multiple users can pin to shared boards. For example, a large public library system with multiple branches could create shared boards while still allowing the branches to maintain their own accounts.

Thornton (2012) found that most academic libraries' Pinterest accounts were primarily focused toward internal audiences of library users and that some familiarity with the library or institution was assumed. The types of material shared on these pinboards ranged from the promotion of libraries, reading, and literacy in general to resource suggestions and highlighting specific library collections and spaces. She emphasizes the importance of preplanning by setting goals and a focus for the library's account. More information about using Pinterest can be found in chapter 5.

Google+

When Google+ launched in 2011, it was widely speculated to be "the Facebook killer," or the service that would eventually overthrow Facebook's dominance as a social media platform. Unfortunately for Google, this has not quite been the case. However, Google+ has still become very popular with some users, and the seamless integration with other Google services is extremely convenient. Google+ may have fewer users overall than Facebook or Twitter, but it has grown much faster than either of these services did initially; thus, it is still an important platform to watch and consider.

Google+ allows users to organize their contacts into "circles" in an effort to replicate the way that real life social networks function. Libraries can organize followers into circles based on their relationship to the library; for example, "Library Staff" and "Patrons," or "Story Time Attendees." Murphy (2011) suggests that libraries could use Google+ Hangouts, a form of videoconferencing, to conduct reference interviews and one-on-one interactions with library users. The Falvey Memorial Library at Villanova University has a Google+ page that features photos and library news (fig. 1.5).

Similar to Facebook, Google+ was slow to allow official organization pages to become part of the system. The "Pages" functionality in Google+ did not become available until several months after the official launch of the service. These pages can be populated with pictures and status updates as well as information about the library. In this way, Google+ pages function similarly to Facebook pages but reach a slightly different audience. Chapter 6 provides information on account setup and best practices for using Google+ as a marketing tool.

FIGURE 1.5
Google+ page for Villanova University Falvey Memorial Library

Foursquare

Foursquare is a platform that ties physical locations into social networking and thus has probably inspired more enthusiastic debate than any other tool discussed in this book. By allowing users to "check in" to physical locations and share this location information on other social networks, Foursquare leverages the combination of global position system (GPS) and map information with social media. Users earn points and receive virtual badges for checking in to certain types of locations, and can become the "mayor" of a particular location by accruing the most check-ins. Businesses and other locations can also offer incentives and deals through Foursquare, such as a discount for checking in or some reward for reaching Mayor status. Although Foursquare was not the first service to do this, it was the first to see widespread success with the model (Rethlefsen 2010).

FIGURE 1.6
Foursquare page for New York Public Library

Libraries can participate in Foursquare by ensuring that the library is listed as a location within the tool and that all information is correct and up to date. Any Foursquare user can create a location to check in to; thus, it is extremely likely that most libraries have a presence on Foursquare whether they know it or not. However, libraries can take this further and add relevant tags within the system, such as *books*, *library*, or *Wi-Fi* (Porter and King 2010); feature tips and to-do lists; or offer incentives to users who check in at the library. Libraries that are hosting large events can create specific check-in options. The New York Public Library Foursquare page (fig. 1.6) contains photos, a map of locations, and tips for particular library branches as well as links to their Twitter and Facebook accounts. Chapter 7 contains more details about using Foursquare for libraries.

Blogs

Blogs are one of the most established social tools on the web and are still incredibly valuable for marketing and outreach. The ability of users to comment on blogs and interact with the library continues to be one of the most valuable features of blogs (Oguz and Holt 2011). Rather than simply publishing static news and press releases, blogs offer the opportunity for users to provide feedback and converse

FIGURE 1.7
Blog page for the Unquiet Library

with the library. Libraries of all types have had success using blogs. Many larger libraries maintain multiple blogs for more specific types of communication, such as blogs devoted to branch libraries or services to children and teens. The Unquiet Library blog (fig. 1.7) is an excellent example of a library blog aimed at teen library users and includes specific information about manners and etiquette for the blog.

There are several common blog platforms used by libraries, with two of the most popular options being Wordpress and Blogger. Blogger is a Google product, and libraries with Google accounts can create blogs using this tool without creating a new account. Wordpress is another popular blog platform that does require the creation of an account. The software is frequently used to power library websites, although the locally-hosted and supported version is a different version than the web-hosted blogging service. However, many librarians may be familiar with the platform in this context and may prefer to use it for this reason. See Chapter 8 for more details on creating and using blogs.

FIGURE 1.8
QR code on an ad for Contra Costa County (CA) Library

QR Codes

Quick-response (QR) codes are scannable, two-dimensional barcodes that contain encoded information. Very popular in Japan where they were developed (Pulliam and Landry 2011), these small black-and-white squares have been steadily entering American life as smartphone ownership increases. QR codes require scanning software to use, which is widely and freely available via smartphone applications. The value in QR codes is their ability to tie the physical world to the virtual. A QR code could be placed on an event flyer, which when scanned would direct a user to more details about the event or to a signup page, or even be used on public transit ads, as shown in figure 1.8.

Dobbs (2011) discusses many ways that she has used QR codes in her school library, such as linking to video tutorials for specific demonstrations and creating links to catalog records for items in the collection. However, she cautions that, at first, many of her students and parents were unfamiliar with what QR codes are and how to use them. An excellent suggestion is to create a QR code with accompanying text that says something such as "What is this barcode?" and instructions for how to scan, which then leads to a page of information about QR codes themselves.

Providence College Library has created a QR Code LibGuide with additional information (Pulliam and Landry 2011). Brigham Young University used twenty-one QR codes to create an audio tour for the library where students scan a particular code and get information for that area of the library (Whitchurch 2011).

QR codes also provide a way to measure the effectiveness of a library's physical marketing materials. Putting a unique QR code on a particular piece of marketing, such as a sign at a bus shelter, allows libraries to measure the number of times that a particular code has been scanned. Of course, more people will see the physical marketing materials than will have the interest or ability to scan the code but QR codes can still provide some evidence toward the effectiveness of these materials for generating further interest. More information about creating and using QR codes is available in Chapter 9.

Twitter

Twitter is a "microblogging" tool that allows user to share "tweets" of 140 characters or less, including spaces, with their followers. The primary challenge of using Twitter is the care with which tweets must be crafted in order to convey useful information in such a short amount of space. In fact, Twitter has been often derided for the abundance of seemingly inane content shared on the service, such as updates about what a particular user is eating for lunch. However, the service has grown into much more than an outlet for status updates and is now a portal for news, innovation, conversation, and more (Rethlefsen 2010). Twitter is very useful for sharing short, factual information as well as links to further information. It is an extremely popular service that many library users are likely already utilizing. Library Twitter accounts can attract an audience beyond just library users. Milstein (2009) suggests that special libraries can often connect with their internal users as well as with enthusiasts for their area of focus.

Twitter can be used to broadcast information from the library and to promote conversations with followers (Milstein 2009). Baylor University has even gone so far as to use Twitter to embed a librarian directly into a course (Young 2011), engaging with students on a real-time basis during their course meetings. This was an extremely effective and rewarding effort, although it did require more time than is generally desirable for most libraries using Twitter. Probably the most well known library on Twitter is the Library of Congress (fig. 1.9), which also has an agreement to archive tweets on the service (Raymond 2010).

FIGURE 1.9
Twitter feed for the Library of Congress

Using a URL shortener such as bit.ly or goo.gl is extremely helpful for libraries on Twitter, as it allows the sharing of links without using as many characters as a full URL might normally take. Twitter also shortens URLs directly within tweets, but they usually look cleaner and more concise if shortened with an external service.

Twitter makes use of hashtags, which are short snippets of text beginning with a hash, or # symbol. Hashtags are easily searchable and allow users to discover tweets on similar topics, such as *election2012* for tweets about the recent U.S. election. Libraries can use hashtags to promote themselves. Hashtags are also particularly effective for promoting specific events.

In addition to general social marketing, Twitter also offers paid advertising. This is primarily through promoted tweets, which are paid advertisements that can either be displayed in users' Twitter feeds or be triggered by a particular search. Chapter 10 provides more information about setting up a Twitter account and using it for marketing.

Other Technologies

The technologies discussed in this book are only a starting point. The sky is the limit when it comes to marketing with technology, from old standbys to hot new social networks that haven't yet hit the mainstream. Do not overlook the potential of the library website which is a marketing platform in its own right and can include promotional materials in a variety of ways. Space on the home page or in banners can be devoted to rotating, graphical advertisements for services and events. LibGuides and other web-based research guides can similarly serve as a marketing platform with an easy-to-update interface and the ability to display multiple content types, including video.

In addition to broader social networks, a number of niche social networks exist based on specific interests. Of particular interest to libraries might be networks of books and reading, such as GoodReads and LibraryThing. Libraries can use these networks to share new and award-winning books and to interact with readers in their area who might not be library users. Other niche networks might also be relevant to libraries depending on their focus, including craft networks such as Ravelry (www.ravelry.com) or scholarly research networks such as Mendeley (www.mendeley.com).

Libraries engaged in capital campaigns or projects that require fundraising may wish to try Kickstarter (www.kickstarter.com) or Peerbackers (www.peerbackers.com), which are social sites that facilitate crowdfunding. Klout (www.klout.com) is a tool that attempts to calculate how much influence a particular user has on certain topics via social media. While this is not exactly scientific, libraries could use this service to get a sense of how much impact their social media presence is having and to identify influential people in their communities to follow and interact with. Lastly, only time will tell whether Myspace (www.myspace.com) is able to successfully reemerge as a dominant social network after falling from prominence in the past few years.

MANAGING AND MONITORING MARKETING TOOLS

When using these or other technologies for marketing, it is important for libraries to provide a regular stream of new content across all of their accounts and services. Libraries look stagnant if they do not follow the norms for a given social media tool, as each tool requires different frequencies of updates. Milstein (2009) recommends, for example, that libraries update their Twitter accounts at least once per day. This may sound daunting initially, but there are tools that can help with the organization and management of social media accounts, including the popular HootSuite (http://hootsuite.com) and TweetDeck (http://tweetdeck.com). These services allow monitoring of multiple accounts, scheduling updates, and monitoring mentions of your library or institution. Hootsuite can manage multiple Twitter, Facebook, LinkedIn, and Foursquare accounts with a single app. There are apps for both Apple and Android devices as well as a web interface. Tweetdeck is for Twitter only, although it provides robust monitoring, filtering, scheduling, and alerts for multiple accounts. The ability to schedule updates in advance is particularly helpful as a time-saving device, as an entire week's or month's worth of content can be planned and scheduled in a single session rather than incorporated into daily workloads.

The services mentioned above provide analytics for accounts connected to the service; however, many of the tools discussed in this book offer robust analytics of their own. Stuart (2009) provides an overview of the types of metrics that various social media platforms provide. Fichter and Wisniewski (2008) recommend framing metrics for success according to library-friendly goals such as "Responsive to patron concerns." Facebook and YouTube, in particular, offer very detailed reports showing how users interact with content on these sites. For services that do not have internal analytics, it is still possible to install an external analytics product, such as Google Analytics, in order to gain more insight into how users are interacting with the service.

In the absence of monitoring or analytics tools, libraries can survey their online reputation by simply listening—not with their ears, but by regularly identifying mentions of the library on social media tools and the rest of the web. Direct mentions of the library's account on services such as Twitter, Facebook, and Pinterest should lead to a notification from the service. These mentions are often compliments, complaints, or requests for simple information. In these instances, a brief reply can engage the library with users, resolve minor issues, or draw attention to excellent service. Of course, direct mentions will not always happen. Periodically searching these services for the library's name in plain text can alert librarians to the ways that their library is being discussed. There are even ways to simplify this process; for example, Google allows for the creation of e-mail alerts, and Twitter allows users to save frequent search terms.

Much of the work involved with managing and monitoring marketing tools, however, depends on the people who are managing these services. It is important to ensure that the staff members assigned to manage these tools have adequate time to do it well and are also the people best suited to update these services based on the marketing plan. For libraries without a dedicated marketing position, this may often fall to web services or public services staff or may be divided among several people. A genuine interest in using the service is helpful; for example, libraries that have a staff member with particular skill and interest in video would be wise to take advantage of this person to manage their YouTube account.

One aspect of using these services that can be rather unpleasant is dealing with negative feedback from users or the public. Unfortunately, the anonymity and sense of removal afforded by the Internet often leads people to engage in offensive and inappropriate behavior. When planning to undertake a marketing effort using technology that encourages feedback, libraries must be prepared to deal with the negative feedback, which may or may not be rational or deserved. Oguz and Holt (2011) provide suggestions for dealing with negative blog comments. It is important to have a plan in place for how the library and the staff managing these tools respond to such feedback. Ideally, libraries should consult with available legal counsel to determine what actions, such as removing Facebook posts or blog comments, may be appropriate. For example, at the UH library, we have been advised by institutional counsel that the university's free speech policies prohibit us from simply deleting negative posts on Facebook.

TIPS FOR SUCCESS

It bears mentioning again the importance of abiding by traditional marketing principles, including consistent branding and messaging across multiple platforms. By utilizing multiple tools, libraries can greatly increase the reach of their marketing efforts, but still risk confusing—and possibly alienating—their users if account names, profile photos, and other branding indicators are inconsistent.

Different types of marketing content work best on different platforms. Obviously video content is well suited to a service such as YouTube or Vimeo, while quick, factual information is most applicable for Twitter or Facebook updates. It is important to think about the types of content the library will be sharing and to identify the most appropriate method for doing so.

Planning ahead for marketing efforts increases the effectiveness and reduces the workload on those staff responsible for implementation. Try to schedule content and updates in advance and automate where possible. Assign responsibilities to those who have the time and interest to implement them effectively, and divide responsibilities among multiple people if necessary and appropriate.

Above all, when utilizing technology for marketing, remember that trial and error is sometimes the best way to determine whether a particular service is a good fit for a particular library's user population. Some user communities connect most naturally with big, established platforms, such as Facebook and Twitter, while others are quick to jump on exciting new platforms, including Pinterest and Foursquare. The more you know about your users, the easier it will be to predict which platforms will resonate with them. Still, there is no magical formula. Sometimes just diving in, creating an account, and simply playing with a new service is the easiest way to determine its value.

REFERENCES

Alcock, Joanne. 2009. "Using Facebook Pages to Reach Users: The Experiences of the University of Wolverhampton." *ALISS Quarterly* 4 (2): 2–6.

Alman, Susan W. 2007. *Crash Course in Marketing for Libraries*. Westport, CT: Libraries Unlimited.

Colburn, Selene, and Laura Haines. 2012. "Measuring Libraries' Use of YouTube as a Promotional Tool: An Exploratory Study and Proposed Best Practices." *Journal of Web Librarianship* 6 (1): 5–31.

Cronin, Kieran, and Terry O'Brien. 2009. "Practical Low-Cost Marketing Measures: The Experience of Waterford Institute of Technology." *New Library World* 110 (11/12): 550–560.

Dobbs, Cherie. 2011. "QR Codes in the Library: It's Not Your Mother's Barcode!" *Library Media Connection* 30 (1): 14–16.

Facebook.com. 2012. "Key Facts." Last updated 2013. http://newsroom.fb.com/Key-Facts.

Falk, Kristen. 2012. "Pinterest." *Library Media Connection* 31 (2): 43.

Fichter, Darlene, and Jeff Wisniewski. 2008. "Social Media Metrics: Making the Case for Making the Effort." *Online* 32 (6): 54–7.

Fredrick, Kathy. 2012. "Sharing Your Library with Facebook Pages." *School Library Monthly* 28 (5): 24–26.

Jackson, Millie, Jonathan Blackburn, and Robert McDonald. 2007. "MediaWiki Open-Source Software as Infrastructure for Electronic Resources Outreach." *The Reference Librarian* 48 (1): 19–36.

Kenneway, Melinda. 2007. "Marketing the Library: Using Technology to Increase Visibility, Impact, and Reader Engagement." *Serials: The Journal for the Serials Community* 20 (2): 92–97.

Little, Geoffrey. 2010. "The Revolution Will Be Streamed Online: Academic Libraries and Video." *The Journal of Academic Librarianship* 37 (1): 70–72.

Mathews, Brian. 2009. *Marketing Today's Academic Library: A Bold New Approach to Communicating with Students.* Chicago: American Library Association.

Milstein, Sarah. 2009. "Twitter for Libraries (and Librarians)." *Computers in Libraries* 29 (5). www.infotoday.com/cilmag/may09/Milstein.shtml.

Moore, Kathleen. 2011. "71% of Online Adults Now Use Video-Sharing Sites." Pew Internet Project. July 25. http://pewinternet.org/Reports/2011/Video-sharing-sites.aspx.

Murphy, Joe. 2011. "Google Plus Pages for Libraries." Joe Murphy—Librarian, Innovator blog. November 9. http://joemurphylibraryfuture.com/google-pages-for-libraries/.

Oguz, Fatih, and Michael Holt. 2011. "Library Blogs and User Participation: A Survey about Comment Spam in Library Blogs." *Library Hi Tech* 29 (1): 173–188.

Porter, Michael, and David Lee King. 2010. "Foursquare for Libraries." *Public Libraries* 49 (2): 22–24.

Pulliam, Beatrice, and Chris Landry. 2011. "Tag, You're It! Using QR Codes to Promote Library Services." *The Reference Librarian* 52 (1/2): 68–74.

Raymond, Matt. 2010. "How Tweet It Is! Library Acquires Entire Twitter Archive." Library of Congress blog. April 14. http://blogs.loc.gov/loc/2010/04/how-tweet-it-is-library-acquires-entire-twitter-archive/.

Rethlefsen, Melissa. 2010. "Checking In: Location Services for Libraries." *Library Journal* 135 (7): 42.

Romero, Nuria Lloret. 2011. "ROI. Measuring the Social Media Return on Investment in a Library." *The Bottom Line: Managing Library Finances* 24 (2): 145–151.

Shontz, Marilyn, Jon C. Parker, and Richard Parker. 2004. "What Do Librarians Think About Marketing? A Survey of Public Librarians' Attitudes toward the Marketing of Library Services." *The Library Quarterly* 74 (1): 63–84.

Stuart, David. 2009. "Social Media Metrics." *Online* 33 (6):22–24.

Stuart, David. 2010. "What Are Libraries Doing on Twitter?" *Online* 34 (1): 45–47.

Thornton, Elaine. 2012. "Is Your Academic Library Pinning? Academic Libraries and Pinterest." *Journal of Web Librarianship* 6 (3): 164–175.

Whitchurch, Michael. 2011. "QR Codes and Library Engagement." *Bulletin of the American Society for Information Science and Technology* 33 (1):14–17.

Young, Jeffrey. 2011. "'Embedded Librarian' on Twitter Served as Information Concierge for Class." *Chronicle of Higher Education*. February 25. http://chronicle.com/blogs/ wiredcampus/embedded-librarian-on-twitter-served-as-information-concierge-for -class/30000.

SUGGESTED READING

General Marketing Principles

Barber, Peggy and Wallace, Linda. 2010. *Building a Buzz: Libraries and Word-of-Mouth Marketing*. Chicago: ALA Editions.
Focuses on word-of-mouth and other unsolicited marketing, with case studies from multiple projects included.

Bunker, L. 2012. "Social Media for Nonprofits and Small Businesses (video). youtube .com/watch?v=BZodTyXE854.
This presentation about using social media effectively, from *Library Journal* Mover & Shaker Lisa Bunker, includes suggestions about best practices for social media and the power of connecting with partners.

Dempsey, Kathy. 2009. *The Accidental Library Marketer*. New Jersey: Information Today.
Particularly helpful for those new to marketing, with information about how to gather data and evaluation of various marketing approaches.

Dowd, Nancy, Mary Evangeliste, and Jonathan Silberman. 2010. *Bite-Sized Marketing: Realistic Solutions for the Overworked Librarian*. Chicago: ALA Editions.
Includes ten marketing strategies suitable for various budgets and audiences, also contains worksheets and other planning aids.

Fisher, Patricia H., and Marseille M. Price. 2009. *Blueprint for Your Library Marketing Plan*. Chicago: American Library Association.
Provides step-by-step instructions for developing a marketing plan, from planning through evaluation.

Hastings, Robin. 2010. *Microblogging and Lifestreaming in Libraries*. New York, NY: Neal-Schuman Publishers.
Offers a good overview of various social networking services that libraries and librarians are using.

King, David Lee. 2012. "Use and Engagement on the Digital Branch." *Library Technology Reports*, 48 (6): 12–15.
This chapter, part of *Running the Digital Branch: Guidelines for Operating the Library Website*, discusses types of user engagement experienced by the digital branch of the Topeka & Shawnee County Public Library, including comments and conversations with library users.

Landis, C. 2010. *A Social Networking Primer for Librarians*. New York: Neal-Schuman.
A stepping stone for both the technical and social sides of social networking.

Mathews, Brian. 2009. *Marketing Today's Academic Library: A Bold New Approach to Communicating with Students.*" Chicago: American Library Association.
Provides a detailed look at marketing strategies, concepts, and terminology focused on the modern academic library, but applicable to other types as well.

Steiner, Sarah K. 2012. *Strategic Planning for Social Media in Libraries.* Chicago, IL: ALA TechSource.
Walks you through the questions to ask yourself up front when setting the plan for your social media strategy.

Zarrella, Dan. 2010. *The Social Media Marketing Book.* Sebastopol, CA: O'Reilly.
Gives an overview of using social media for marketing campaigns.

Getting Started with Social Media Tools

Ballard, Terry. 2012. *Google This! Putting Google and Other Social Media Sites to Work for Your Library.* Oxford: Chandos Publishing.
Discusses building and maintaining social media and other web presence, with a focus on Google products, although others are included.

Crawford, Walt. 2012. *Successful Social Networking in Public Libraries.* Chicago: ALA Editions.
Analyzes social network uses by a variety of libraries in both type and size.

Del Bosque, Darcy, S. Lief, and Susie Skarl. 2012. "Libraries Atwitter: Trends in Academic Library Tweeting." *Reference Services Review* 40 (2): 199–213.
This study examines how academic libraries are using Twitter.

Li, C., and J. Bernoff. 2011. *Groundswell, Expanded and Revised Edition: Winning in a World Transformed by Social Technologies.* Boston, MA: Harvard Business Review Press.
The chapter "Tapping the Groundswell with Twitter" describes marketing objectives for Twitter, including listening, talking, energizing, supporting, and embracing. While oriented toward businesses, the lessons and examples included are interesting reading for libraries as well.

Solomon, Laura. 2010. *Doing Social Media So It Matters: A Librarian's Guide.* Chicago: ALA Editions.
Short but powerful book that is excellent for those new to social media, with many positive and negative examples of social media use.

Steiner, Sarah K. 2012. *Strategic Planning For Social Media In Libraries.* Chicago: ALA TechSource.
Focused on social media strategy and outcomes over using particular tools, with exercises to help libraries create their own plans.

Sump-Crethar, A. N. 2012. "Making the Most of Twitter." *The Reference Librarian* 53 (4): 349–354.
Offers additional ideas for using and managing Twitter for your library.

Keeping Current with Marketing Technologies

ALA TechSource (blog). www.alatechsource.org

Beth's Blog: How Nonprofits Can Use Social Media. www.bethkanter.org

Library Success: A Best Practices Wiki. www.libsuccess.org

Mashable. www.mashable.com

"Twitter for Business." https://business.twitter.com/

The "M" Word: Marketing Libraries (blog). www.themword.blogspot.com

Wired. www.wired.com

Using Facebook to Market Libraries

Mindy Tomlin, University of Texas at Tyler

Facebook, one of the most common social networking sites, has exploded to the point of dominating web usage since its creation in 2004. According to Alexa .com (2012), Facebook is the second most visited website in the world following Google. As of October 4, 2012, Facebook had one billion monthly active users, and in September 2012, the site had 584 million daily active users (Etherington 2012). Users vary in age, sex, socioeconomic status, religion, and various other facets of life, thus making Facebook a viable option to engage a large portion of library users in an environment they are already using. With this level of usage in mind, it is not a question of whether or not to embrace Facebook but how to proceed with an implementation that will reach as many patrons as possible.

During the early years of Facebook, the site was limited only to students—first college and then high school—a process that was validated through institutional e-mail accounts. The popularity of the site quickly grew, and by 2006, all users were welcome to join (Phillips 2007). Institutional profiles were regulated to "Groups" pages until November 2007, when the site introduced Facebook pages. The "Pages" feature essentially acts as a profile for organizations or institutions to promote their presence: bands, sports teams, artists, films, brands, nonprofits, and businesses (Facebook 2012).

While Facebook is not a new technology, it still can pose some challenges for libraries. Although many libraries have experimented with Facebook, there are questions about how to improve a presence in order to better provide services to patrons. Common questions include: "What types of things should I post?" "How do I get more likes?" This chapter seeks to provide groundwork for institutions that have not yet established a Facebook presence and also to provide tips on enhancing and sustaining a successful one.

FACEBOOK FOR MARKETING

There are several steps that are important to create an effective marketing Facebook page. The sections below will guide you through the process.

Establishing an Account

Facebook has two primary options for libraries seeking to communicate with users: groups and pages. This chapter will focus on using pages, due to the additional assessment features pages offer. Both pages and groups can be created and managed from personal or organization accounts.

Groups

Groups are small, personalized spaces for people with shared interests and can be created by anyone. Members of a given group add other members and users have control over privacy settings on posts. Members are also able to post documents, create and share events, and participate in chats. One of the major limitations of groups is that administrators are not able to send messages to members once the group reaches five thousand members (Smarty 2010).

Users can create a group using the home page of Facebook. In the left column of the page is a section "Groups." At the bottom of the section is a link, "Create Group." To create a group, select this link. Selecting it brings up a form to input information on the group. Name the group and select members to immediately add to the group. From there, select the privacy settings: open (open to anyone), closed (nonmembers can view who is in the group, but only members can see the posts), or secret (only members can see the group, other members, and posts).

Once the basic information is filled out, a box to choose an icon for the group will appear. This step is optional. Once an icon is chosen, the group is created. The home page for a group allows members to post, add photos/videos, create polls, and add files to the wall (fig. 2.1). The "About" page provides a description of the group, along with a list of members. The group page also has tabs for events, photos, and files, respectively. It is not currently possible to convert a Facebook

FIGURE 2.1
Sample Facebook group page

group into a Facebook page. Libraries with groups may, however, create a page and notify group members (Facebook 2012).

Pages

Facebook pages have several features similar to personal profiles: users can add apps, post stories, host events, and much more. Pages are public and can be viewed by anyone on Facebook. Any user can like a page, an action that subscribes them to updates from the page. There are no limits to the number of likes a page can receive. Pages have various levels of administrators who can post or respond to users on the page's behalf. One of the most useful features of pages is the "Insights" feature, which tracks a page's growth, activity, user demographics, and more. This feature is discussed in further detail below.

To create a page, search the "Help" menu, search *create Facebook page* on the web, or go directly to the "Create a Page" screen: https://www.facebook.com/pages/create.php. On this screen, select "Company, Organization, or Institution" to get started. Choose a category and a company name, and agree to the Facebook pages terms.

Finding Followers

Once your page has been created, the next step is to build a fan base by inviting followers. One way to do this is to contact potential followers via e-mail. From the admin panel, go to "Build Audience" and select "Invite Email Contacts." From there, choose one of the e-mail services and import references. If your e-mail service is not supported, go to "Other Email Service," enter an e-mail address, and select "Invite Contacts." Outlook Express, Thunderbird, Apple Mail, and more are listed

27

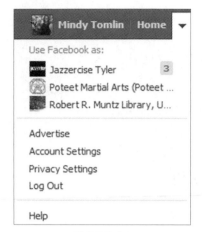

FIGURE 2.2
Changing the Facebook
page voice

under "Other Tools." This option requires creating a contact file. Note that the "E-mail Contacts" feature is limited to a maximum of five thousand contacts.

Another way to increase followers is to like and interact with other pages (Guza 2011). While any social media is a very useful tool to simply broadcast events, services, and library tools, Facebook is a very social tool. Use it to create discussions within your fan base in addition to announcing events and library resources and services. Bear in mind that social networks are intrinsically built on social capital, which requires time to build in any given community. Liking and interacting with posts from other pages helps build social capital (Solomon 2011). This can be done by changing the voice. From the drop-down menu in the top right of your profile, go to "Use Facebook As" and select your library's page, as shown in figure 2.2. With this option, any one page can like other pages and can interact with users.

A marketing campaign outside of Facebook is another way to increase followers. Once your library's page is established and a custom web address is generated, add the address to marketing materials: brochures, newsletters, websites, and any other tools the library has available, such as Ask-a-Librarian services. On a smaller scale, include the address on e-mail signature lines and ask staff to promote the page during events and classes.

Recently, Facebook introduced the option to pay for featured advertisements. This is a more aggressive marketing campaign that can target Facebook users who are not connected with your page. However, it is not necessary to use advertisements in order to create a successful and robust Facebook page.

Staffing the Service

Creating and implementing a social media campaign is a time consuming process that requires continuous maintenance and is often easiest when shared among several people (Guza 2011). Ideally there will be several people interested in social media at your library who can post to the Facebook page. Pages allow for an unlimited number of admins with varying responsibility—see Facebook for details.

When selecting page administrators, keep the following in mind:

- Try to have at least a few people in both the manager and the content creator roles. Many campuses, cities, and schools have some type of news or marketing department. These departments will likely need to be in a manager role, along with the library director and/or marketing contact. Having multiple people in these roles will ensure access and knowledge in the event of staff turnover.
- If several people are involved in posting, establish a best practices or style guide for administrators to follow. This will help ensure stylistic consistency and is a useful part of a procedures document, even if a single person is responsible for all the posts.
- Include content creators from several departments to add diversity to the types of posts.
- Recruit staff with a genuine interest in social media and who have the willingness to spend time posting, responding, and learning new features. Social media is a rapidly changing technology, and Facebook is no exception.

29

MAINTAINING FACEBOOK FOR MARKETING

Establishing and keeping a Facebook page actively marketing your library's resources requires regular monitoring, continual updating, and frequent enhancing. The sections below provide details on these activities.

Monitoring

The admin panel is one of the most useful and powerful features of pages and is the primary tool for monitoring pages. The panel is broken down into several components: notifications (which contains new activity such as likes or comments on posts), messages, new likes to the page, the "Insights" feature, and page tips. Figure 2.3 demonstrates these options.

Prompt turnaround and responses to comments are vital, especially in an online environment. Staff should monitor the panel daily to ensure quick responses to virtual followers. It is also possible to enable e-mail notifications for administrators. On your page, select the "Edit Page" button above the admin panel and select "Manage Notifications" (fig. 2.4). Make sure the option to send e-mails when the page receives new activity is checked and select "Save."

FIGURE 2.3
Facebook admin panel

Updating

When posting, remember to maintain a professional presence with a human element. Facebook is a casual way for people to connect and using stiff business language can unintentionally alienate patrons. Try to "foster conversation, ask for opinions, involve your stakeholders, and share content across multiple platforms when possible. You can still use social media

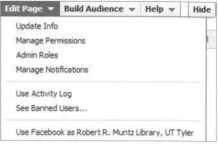

FIGURE 2.4
Managing notifications on Facebook

as a marketing platform, but don't use it solely for outgoing marketing messages" (Steiner 2012, 86). Listed below are a few ways to make posts more personable and user-friendly:

- Have staff sign off with their name to give the post a more personal approach. For example: *Check out today's book reading with free cookies. Hope to see you there! /Mindy*
- Before posting, consider what you want the user to get from the post. For example, rather than posting, "Writing Center at the library on Tuesdays

and Thursdays, 8–10 pm," try the following: "Can't figure out how to format your essay? Come talk to the Writing Center tutors in the library this Thursday between 8 and 10 pm". For more tips on posts, see Solomon (2011).

- Ask followers questions—such as "Where is your favorite spot to study in the library?"—in order to encourage conversation. Assign someone to respond to questions in a timely manner.
- Post more than just text. Videos, infographics, links, polls, pictures, and other forms of media provide diversity and are more interesting and engaging than text alone.

Regular posting is one of the best ways to ensure that a page remains in fan feeds. Facebook recommends posting to a page at least once per week, although posting more often will help increase activity. The frequency of posting is dependent on your target audience. Aim for at least several posts per week, with daily being preferable. There are several tools that can be used to schedule posts, including Hoot-Suite (www.hootesuite .com) or the "Schedule" feature embedded into Facebook.

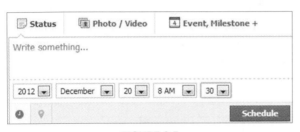

FIGURE 2.5
Scheduling a post on Facebook

To access the "Schedule" feature of Facebook, go to your page wall. Select the clock icon on the lower left-hand side of the status, and then fill in the year, month, day, and time for the post to appear. (This process is demonstrated in fig. 2.5.) Posts can be scheduled six months in the future and can also be backdated. If a post is backdated, it will automatically appear in the appropriate place on the page timeline.

Enhancing

One of the simplest ways to enhance a page is by filling out as much of the information as possible that is already embedded into the page. For example, create a thorough profile complete with contact and hours information to improve search results. Additionally, choose unique photographs for profile and cover images.

Adding pictures to the photo albums also provides a fun way for followers to interact with the library. In addition to posting pictures of events, try posting images of displays, historical photos (if the library has an archives or genealogy department), covers of featured books, snapshots of staff in action, and more. Frequent posting to albums also provides an opportunity to chronicle the library's history and events.

Facebook also offers several applications, or apps, which can embed other information in your page. Consider using these apps to link out to or sync with other social media. If your library has a presence on Twitter, YouTube, or a blog, be sure to link these resources for maximum exposure. Several free tools exist to make the insertion of apps easier:

- thruSocial (http://thrusocial.com) has a drag and drop interface, allowing you to pull from other major social media resources such as YouTube, WordPress, and more. Note that some widgets require a paid account.
- Involver (www.involver.com) allows users to select two apps for free, which is useful for embedding a Twitter or YouTube feed into a page.

Additional free, legitimate tools are also available. When searching through pages for other libraries and businesses, check their apps. Scroll to the bottom of the page and search for a "powered by" logo which will direct you to the resource (Ekhart 2011).

EVALUATING, ASSESSING, AND USING STATISTICS

The "Insights" feature of Facebook offers several assessment tools to assist with evaluating Page usage. As well as providing basic information, such as the number of likes, people talking about posts, and information on the reach of a page, "Insights" also offers information on the demographics of page fans. Detailed information on "Insights" is available from the admin panel by selecting "See All" (fig. 2.6). The data can also be exported to XLS and CSV file formats for later use.

A written strategy, which includes evaluation and assessment, helps ensure success (Guza 2011). Several factors should be considered when evaluating your page usage. Create a list of goals for your social media tools, including Facebook. The strategic plan for an institution and their mission statement are good places to seek inspiration. This step is vital to determine which metrics will be used for future evaluation. Consider some of the following potential goals:

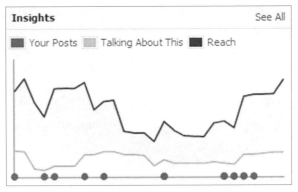

FIGURE 2.6
Facebook Insights on the admin panel

- Increase attendance at events
- Improve awareness of your library
- Improve your library's online and overall reputation

Once the assessment strategy is developed, establish a baseline measurement and determine the frequency of evaluation. Building a social presence takes time. It is highly unlikely that a page will have several hundred likes within a week or even a few months. If your page is stagnant or receives consistent negative feedback for an extended period of time, evaluate posting practices. Is it only information to the library's events? Are other organizations' events and activities posted (city departments, campus and school events, for example)? How frequently is content posted? What type of content is posted? Are user comments and messages promptly acknowledged and answered? Try adjusting your strategy, content, and timeframe for more success.

▩ CASE STUDIES ▩

University of Texas at Tyler Zombrarians

In the spring of 2012, the Robert R. Muntz Library at the University of Texas at Tyler implemented a "Zombrarian" team to actively participate in Humans versus Zombies, which is a campus-wide alternate reality game run by students. The game was conducted through Facebook groups and pages, with game players receiving communication through their personal Facebook feeds. Zombrarians posted promotional materials on behalf of the library within the group, although they were careful to abstain from posting too much in order to avoid overwhelming or alienating students. Promotional materials included an online zombie survival guide, flyers promoting the library's social media activity throughout the week, and a zombie-themed book display. Once students spotted some of the library's promotional and outreach materials online and around campus, they began taking pictures and reposting information within the group and on their own personal feeds (fig. 2.7).

FIGURE 2.7
Student posting of print marketing materials,
Robert R. Muntz Library, University of Texas at Tyler

Zombrarians interacted with the Humans versus Zombies group through their own personal Facebook profiles. As representatives of the library, staff made sure posts were professional and personable. Discussion of the tone used on social media should be addressed in the preliminary stages of planning and include recommendations in a best practices or style guide.

Seattle Public Library

With over seventeen thousand likes, the Seattle Public Library (SPL) is one of the best examples of library marketing through Facebook. The SPL has a dedicated Social Media Team comprised of members from several library departments at the central library and hopes to expand to the branch libraries in the future (Robinson, Thomas, and Ullman 2011). The team has drastically increased their Facebook following, and fans regularly interact with the library through postings.

The team monitors the page seven days a week during regular operating hours. Postings are on a variety of topics: services, events, images of library displays and unique holdings, videos of librarians recommending materials, relevant web articles, reading lists, and much more. The library also makes sure that their posts are personable and often inject humor into posts. Figure 2.8 features a post designed to start conversation; it received over forty comments and more than a hundred likes. Additionally, the team regularly asks questions of users and posts polls to get conversations started on their page.

35

FIGURE 2.8
Facebook picture and post plus comments, Seattle Public Library

FIGURE 2.9
Facebook post featuring a readers' advisory event,
Seattle Public Library

In addition to regularly posting a variety of materials and creating an engaging space for patrons to interact, the Seattle Public Library has embraced Facebook as a way to actively promote public services, especially readers' advisory. On November 14, 2012, a team of six Seattle librarians monitored Facebook from 10 am to 8 pm and encouraged patrons to share their favorite books. Librarians in turn responded with personalized book recommendations (fig. 2.9). In the November 2012 event, novelist Maria Semple and Mary Ann Gwinn, books editor of the *Seattle Times*, assisted with the event through Facebook access.

Seattle Public Library's Social Media Team organizes their materials, ideas, and postings through an intranet (Robinson, Thomas, and Ulman 2011). Team members send in potential posts and receive feedback from other members of the team. The team uses Google Calendars to schedule when posts go up to ensure consistency and reduced duplication in posts. The use of the intranet allows for documentation in the event of staff turnover or absence. For example, if a member of the team is out sick, posting still continues.

A general privacy notice on SPL's website covers online interactions with the library, including expectations of the library staff and patrons. This policy is written in clear, nontechnical language and frees the library from any liability. The open nature of the policy allows for variations in types of social media. Early on, the Social Media Team set a goal of transparency in their postings and decided not to remove negative comments, choosing instead to address them directly on the page. The only content that the team removes is spam and commercial posts.

■ ■ ■

BEST PRACTICES AND CONCLUSIONS

As previously mentioned, the nature of Facebook is one of immediacy as followers want and expect quick responses to comments; institutions must update on a regular basis to maintain relevancy. This can be a time-consuming process, particularly as the number of followers increases. To ease this burden, multiple people should be recruited to assist with the monitoring of Facebook, and a schedule needs to be established for posting and monitoring.

When creating a schedule, consider what content is needed and when posting should take place. Are there several events going on during a single day? If so, try to spread out posts rather than putting them all up at once. If necessary, space out posts over the course of several hours or days. Sending out too many posts at once gives the impression of spamming and can alienate followers. Spreading out posts also ensures constant posting rather than letting a page linger without updates for several days. Keep your social media goals at the forefront of all posts. Before each posting, think about what benefit the users will get out of it. If the answer is unclear, revise the post or consider omitting it (Solomon 2011).

As with other forms of social media, Facebook changes at a rapid pace. One of the keys to success is to stay informed of updates and changes. This can be done through a number of methods, including following official Facebook updates on their page and following technology blogs, such as Mashable.com. By remaining flexible and adaptive, your institution will be able to fully embrace the functionality of Facebook and reach out to patrons through this tool.

REFERENCES

Alexa.com. 2012. "Top Sites." www.alexa.com/topsites.

Ekhart, Donna F. 2011. "Tech Tips for Every Librarian." *Computers in Libraries* 31 (September): 46–47.

37

Etherington, Darrell. 2012. "Facebook Tops 1 billion Active Users." TechCrunch. October 12. http://techcrunch.com/2012/10/04/facebook-tops-1-billion-monthly-users-ceo-mark-zuckerberg-shares-a-personal-note/.

Guza, Tracy. 2011. "Washington Libraries Reveal Social Media Secrets". *Alki* 27 (March): 19–21.

Phillips, Sarah. 2007. "A Brief History of Facebook." *Guardian*. July 25. www.theguardian.com/technology/2007/jul/25/media.newmedia.

Robinson, Jennifer, Toby Thomas, and Caroline Ullman. 2011. "Connecting with Your Community via Facebook: They Already Like You!" Webinar presented by the Texas State Library. http://librariansbuildcommunities.wordpress.com/2011/07/05/connecting-with-your-community-via-facebook-they-already-like-you/.

Smarty, Ann. 2010. "3 Facebook Limitations You as a Marketer Should Be Aware Of." Search Engine Journal. August 23. www.searchenginejournal.com/3-facebook-limitations-you-as-a-marketer-should-be-aware-of/23469/.

Solomon, Laura. 2011. *Doing Social Media So It Matters: A Librarian's Guide*. Chicago: American Library Association.

Steiner, Sarah K. 2012. *Strategic Planning for Social Media in Libraries*. Chicago: ALA TechSource.

Using Wikis to Market Services and Resources

Megan Kocher, University of Minnesota

Wikis were invented in 1995 by Ward Cunningham to serve his own needs for a collaborative online workspace for programmers. *Wiki* is the Hawaiian term for "quick," and Cunningham's WikiWikiWeb was a place where users could quickly create, edit, and collaborate on web pages using a simplified markup language (Abell 2010). By 2007, it was estimated that 44 percent of U.S. citizens between the ages of 18 and 29 looked for information on Wikipedia (Rainie and Tancer 2007), and hundreds of different wiki software products and applications existed that allowed users to create wikis that suited their purposes and budgets. Libraries were quick to experiment with using wikis, both internally and publicly. Wikis offer libraries the following advantages over other types of technologies such as blogs and websites:

- Agility: Wikis allow users to create, edit, link, and delete pages quickly, without uploading them to a server or going through a web administrator.
- Ease of editing: Early wikis required users to learn wiki markup language, a simplified version of HTML. Currently, many wikis employ WYSIWYG (what you see is what you get) editors that do not require any knowledge of markup language.
- Collaboration: Wiki pages are not static. They are designed to allow multiple users to edit and build upon what is already there, while still archiving past versions for ease of reversion if necessary. The foremost example of this, of course, is the crowd-sourced online encyclopedia Wikipedia.

- Control of access: While wikis let any user add and edit content, they do not have to be open to everyone on the Internet. Wikis allow administrators to determine whether they will be open to everyone or to a set group of users, such as in the case of a staff intranet or a group project.

This chapter will examine the popular wiki softwares, offer advice for choosing software, provide an example of initial account creation, and discuss best practices for setting up and maintaining a library wiki for marketing. Several case studies are included as examples.

TOP WIKI SOFTWARE

There are many options to consider when choosing a wiki software or application. Two online resources that provide a comparison of different wikis based on their features and functionality are WikiMatrix (www.wikimatrix.org) and Wikipedia's "Comparison of Wiki Software" entry (http://en.wikipedia.org/wiki/Comparison_of_Wiki_software). The first decision that needs to be made, though, is whether to use a wiki that is hosted by a third party (vendor), or one that will be hosted locally by your institution or on a personal server. This decision is often dependent on the purpose of the wiki and will determine which types of software are available for review.

Third-Party Hosted Wikis

Vendor-hosted wikis offer the advantages of not requiring server space or technical expertise for installation. In addition, they usually do not need to be backed up locally, as this is usually also handled by the vendor. A con of third-party hosted wikis is that, as with any third-party solution, you are at the mercy of the vendor; thus, it is important to choose a host who is likely to be around for as long as you would like to have access to the wiki. In addition, some vendor-hosted wikis, especially free ones, place advertisements on users' wiki pages. These types of wikis can be difficult to migrate to other platforms if you need to move your content elsewhere. The following third-party hosted wikis are recommended for librarians and educators:

PBWorks

http://pbworks.com/

Pressley (2010) recommends PBWorks because it is easy to use and is targeted specifically toward the education market. PBWorks offers enterprise-wide solutions, most of which come at a fee, as well as free personal wikis for noncommercial use.

Wikispaces

www.wikispaces.com

Wikispaces wikis are widely used by school librarians as a home page for their library. The Beaufort Academy Library website, shown in figure 3.1, is a good example of this use. Wikispaces offers free and paid plans for educators depending on the level of storage space, branding, and functionality needed.

Google Sites

https://sites.google.com

Although it is not technically a wiki per se, Google Sites bears mentioning, as it offers many of the same features as third-party hosted wikis. Google Sites allow users to create free collaborative web spaces using a

41

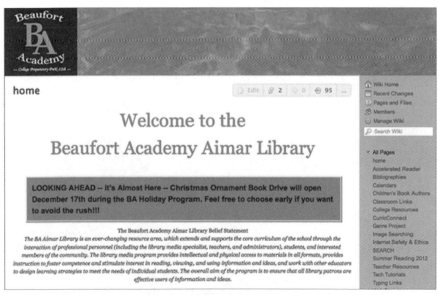

FIGURE 3.1
Wikispaces page for Beaufort Academy Aimar Library

WYSIWYG editor. These sites can be open or private. Many institutions are turning to Google Apps and Google Apps for Education as system-wide tools; thus, Google Sites is a viable option to create a wiki-like environment. The Unquiet Library, https://sites.google.com/site/theun quietlibrary/home, is one example of a website that has transitioned from Wikispaces to Google Sites.

Locally Hosted Wikis

Locally hosted wikis are appealing because they offer users more control over how their wiki is set up and implemented. The software is also free of ads, and many are free to download as open-source software. Locally hosted wikis are particularly useful if you are planning a large wiki project that will have many pages and users, such as a staff intranet or a system-wide solution for creating subject guides. It is important to keep in mind when choosing this option that although the software may be free, it requires a significant amount of staff time and expertise for the initial setup as well as the ongoing maintenance and updates. This also requires that your institution have its own stable, supported server space on which to host the wiki. When choosing a locally hosted wiki product, Pressley (2010) recommends taking into account:

- how popular the software is
- how active the developer community is
- the strengths and functionality that the software offers

Three of the top locally hosted wiki softwares used by libraries are:

MediaWiki
www.mediawiki.org/wiki/MediaWiki

MediaWiki is open source and free to download. It was originally developed to host Wikipedia and, because of this connection, it is a long-standing and well-supported product. In a 2009 study of academic libraries using wikis, Kai-Wah Chu (2009) found that MediaWiki was the most commonly used wiki software among these types of libraries and recommends it for others due to the stability, ability to handle a great deal of content, and ease of installation. The Ohio State University Japanese Studies subject guide, shown in figure 3.3, is a great example of a MediaWiki page.

Tiki

http://info.tiki.org/tiki-index.php

> Another open-source, free wiki software, Tiki is unique in that it boasts some of the most frequently built-in features, including social networking components (polls, chat, comments, etc.), e-learning tools (quizzes, webinars, etc.), and personal information management (calendars, address books, time sheets, etc.). While not yet as popular as some other software, the availability of these features makes Tiki an important wiki to consider, especially if you are seeking maximum socialization with your users.

PMWiki

www.pmwiki.org

> On the PMWiki Success Stories website (www.pmwiki.org/wiki/PmWiki/ SuccessStories), the University of Minnesota Libraries are quoted as saying they chose PMWiki as the software for their internal staff wiki, shown in the "Case Studies" section, "because of its clear philosophy, clear documentation, and active user community." PMWiki is also open source and free to download. Pressley (2010) notes that PMWiki's feature set is very basic, although more functions can be acquired through add-ons.

43

ESTABLISHING AN ACCOUNT

For demonstration purposes, this chapter will use Wikispaces as an example for establishing a wiki account. The steps are listed below:

1. Because Wikispaces offers different types of accounts for different types of uses, you must first choose between education, business, and personal accounts by choosing one of the labeled boxes at the top of the screen. Both education and personal accounts have free and for-pay options. In this example, we will create an education account. There are various options within this category for teachers, students, K–12, and higher education. The choice at this stage depends on whether you are planning to set up your wiki account as an individual educator or as an institution. We will select "Teachers" here to set up an individual account.

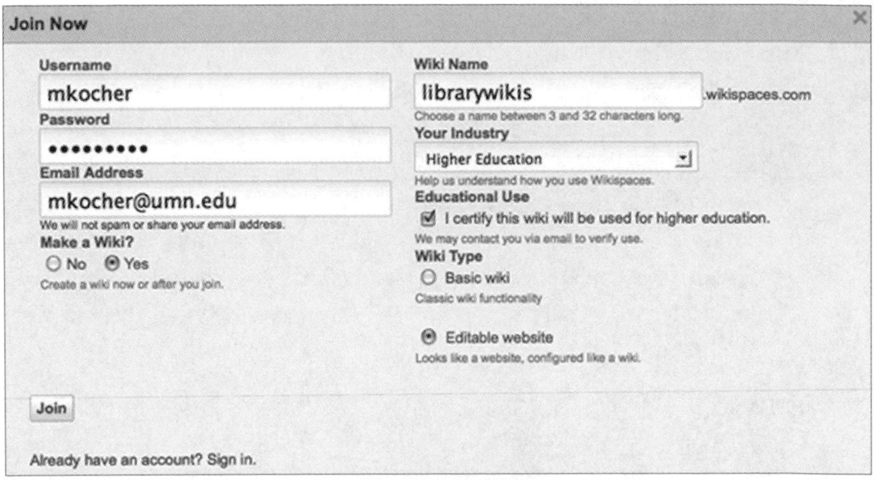

FIGURE 3.2
Wikispaces "Join Now" screen

2. After selecting "Teachers," you are prompted to "Sign up and start your wiki." This requires filling out a short form (fig. 3.2) including the "Wiki Name," which will be part of your wiki's URL, and "Wiki Type," which determines whether you would like a basic wiki setup or a website that is configured like a wiki.

3. After completing the form, you are taken to your new wiki site and offered the option of a virtual tour of the Wikispaces system. Click "Edit" to begin changing the content on your home page, or use the wiki control panel on the right to add pages and files and add members. Selecting "Manage Wiki" allows you to edit your wiki settings as well as to change the look and feel by selecting a theme and/or adding a logo.

DEVELOPING NAVIGATION

With any website, it is important to develop navigation that is uncluttered, free of jargon, and easy to follow. Most wiki products have some form of global navigation built in, allowing the user to navigate from one page to the home page or to any other page on the site. However, even with the constrictions of these built-in navigation systems, it is usually possible to do some custom configuration. In Wikispaces, for example, site administrators are given the options to show all pages in a wiki in the right-hand navigation column, to show pages grouped by tags, or not to show any pages in the navigation bar at all. Showing all pages in the navigation may be the simplest way for users to follow along if there are relatively few pages. With larger wikis, however, it may make more sense either to group pages by tags or to develop your own navigation using some pages to link to others. You may also want to consider developing an internal navigation system to guide users in jumping to different parts of the page if you have one long page.

ADDING AND MAINTAINING CONTENT

Adding content is as simple as clicking the "Edit" button and typing once the wiki is established. Most wikis are equipped with a text editor that allows users to enter text in different fonts, colors, and styles, as well as to embed pictures, create lists, and link to other websites. These websites can be either within the same wiki or anywhere on the Internet. If multiple people will be contributing to the wiki, it is important to assess the users' level of comfort with working in this type of environment and to provide training or written instructions in order to facilitate effective participation (Pressley 2010).

Maintaining the wiki is crucial and requires the development of a maintenance plan. A wiki site promoting outdated information and resources reflects poorly on an institution as well as the individuals responsible, and frequently has the opposite effect of what was originally intended. Pressley (2010) suggests assigning specific people within an organization to check wiki content periodically for currency. If you are the sole maintainer of your wiki site, the maintenance plan may be as simple as setting up quarterly reminders for yourself to check wiki content. If you are hosting your wiki locally, another maintenance issue is keeping the software up to date. Technical staff time needs to be budgeted to keep up with this throughout the lifetime of the wiki.

EVALUATING, ASSESSING, AND USING STATISTICS

Having a well-formed plan to evaluate and assess the wiki is vital. The plan will help you determine whether to continue with the wiki if you are using it as a pilot project, let you know if your intention for the wiki has been successful, and provide you with information that will inform your marketing and promotion efforts.

As an example, if a wiki is used as a subject guide, important measures include the number of visits to the site, where page traffic comes from, and whether your resources are used. There may be some analytic tools included in the wiki feature set. If one is not available or is insufficient for your needs, look into installing a site visit widget on your wiki or using another analytics tool, such as Google Analytics. Locally hosted wikis are usually easy to add on to while vendor-hosted wikis may require special permissions.

If you are using a wiki to interact with users, valuable measures of the wiki's success include whether or not people engage with it, add comments, and make edits of their own. If the wiki is being used with a specific group of people, such as a class, a survey can be employed to gauge the wiki's usefulness and the users' level of involvement. Similarly, a wiki for library staff can be assessed based on whether staff use and contribute to the wiki. Page revision histories can be mined for this information. Surveys and focus groups are also useful tools for assessment.

CASE STUDIES

The flexibility of wikis enables libraries to showcase their services and resources to a variety of audiences using multiple methods. One example of this is wikis that are used as subject or resource guides. Figure 3.3 shows the Ohio State University Libraries' subject guide for Japanese Studies.

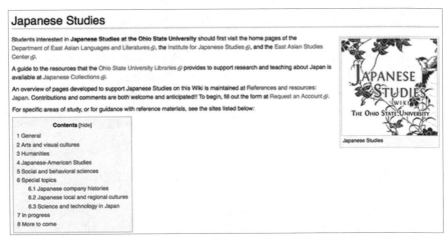

FIGURE 3.3
Japanese Studies wiki, Ohio State University Libraries

When used as subject guides, wikis allow multiple librarians to collaborate on adding the best resources in a particular area. Wikis are easy to edit, allowing resources to be added or removed at any time, thus ensuring that the best information is available for users. In the case of the Japanese Studies guide, information is kept up to date by work-study students (M. Donovan, personal communication, November 28, 2012).

Due to their collaborative nature, wikis can also be used to engage users with library resources. Clarke and Coyle (2011) describe creating a "wiki knowledge base" tied to a particular course using the wiki functionality of the Blackboard course management system. This knowledge base allowed librarians and subject experts to compile a list of resources and make them available to the students and professors who could benefit from them. In addition, students were able to add resources to the wiki when they found useful items that were not already listed, thereby increasing the wiki's value in terms of relevance and promoting student engagement with library resources. Other possibilities for engaging users with library resources include creating collaborative writing spaces (Germain 2008), using a wiki for patron book reviews, and allowing patrons to leave feedback on reference sources using a wiki (Bejune 2007).

One of the most common uses of wikis in libraries is as a staff intranet. This allows all staff to add knowledge and resources to the wiki while learning from one another so that they are better able to promote resources to patrons. A librarian from the University of Toronto describes using their Engineering & Computer Science Library reference desk wiki "as a collaborative space to share knowledge, provide each other with support on challenging reference questions, post exercises

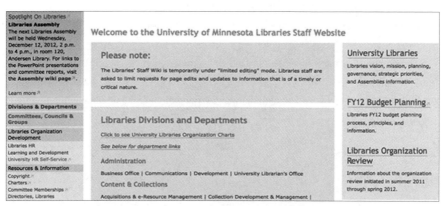

FIGURE 3.4
University of Minnesota Libraries staff wiki

for staff being trained, and to provide heads-ups on major assignments for which we'll get questions" (C. Sewerin, personal communication, November 20, 2012). An example of the University of Minnesota Libraries' internal staff wiki is shown in figure 3.4. This wiki is used for communication and resource sharing across departments and units in this large, spread-out library system.

BEST PRACTICES AND CONCLUSIONS

Your wiki will market your services and resources—but you need to remember to market your wiki. Introducing your wiki in a systematic way to users can help ensure that it makes an impact and gets used effectively. For example, Jeffery and Dworak (2010) recommend keeping staff up to date on wiki developments using regular e-mail communications and holding a series of in-person staff trainings when rolling out a wiki for library staff. They suggest timing the introduction of the wiki so that it does not coincide with other big technology implementations and stress the importance of communicating the purpose of the wiki and needs that it will fill to get user buy-in.

Pressley (2010) gives some more tips for marketing a wiki, including:

- Post flyers and signage.
- Develop bookmarks and takeaways.
- Place the wiki prominently on your website.
- Set the wiki as the home page on library computers.
- Incorporate social networking and Web 2.0 sites.
- Target a few key players who can influence others.

The marketing plan—together with your content, maintenance, and assessment plans—will give your wiki the best chance of reaching its audience and showcasing your valuable services and resources. You, in turn, will have an easily updated, collaborative workspace for your staff and patrons.

REFERENCES

Abell, J. C. 2010. "March 25, 1995: First Wiki Makes Fast Work of Collaboration." *Wired: This Day in Tech* (blog). March 25. www.wired.com/thisdayintech/2010/03/0325wiki wikiweb-first-wiki/.

Bejune, M. M. 2007. "Wikis in Libraries." *Information Technology and Libraries* 26 (3): 26–38.

Clarke, James B., and James R. Coyle. 2011. "A Capstone Wiki Knowledge Base: A Case Study of an Online Tool Designed to Promote Life-Long Learning through Engineering Literature Research." *Issues in Science & Technology Librarianship* 65 (Spring): 1–14.

Germain, C. A. 2008. "Marketing 2.0." *Public Services Quarterly* 4 (2): 169–174.

Jeffery, Keven, and Ellie Dworak. 2010. "Who Moved My Intranet? The Human Side of Introducing Collaborative Technologies to Library Staff." *Journal of Web Librarianship* 4 (2/3): 177–186.

Kai-Wah Chu, S. 2009. "Using Wikis in Academic Libraries." *The Journal of Academic Librarianship* 35 (2): 170–176.

Pressley, Lauren. 2010. *Wikis for Libraries*. New York: Neal-Schuman Publishers.

Rainie, L., and B. Tancer. 2007. "Wikipedia Users." Pew Internet & American Life Project, 1–7. www.pewinternet.org/Reports/2007/Wikipedia-users.aspx.

Using Video-Sharing Sites to Market Your Library

Katie Buehner, University of Houston Libraries

In 2010, the Harold B. Lee Library (HBLL) Multimedia Production Unit, Brigham Young University, uploaded the video "Study Like a Scholar, Scholar" to the popular video-sharing site YouTube. The video parodied a series of Old Spice commercials—"The Man Your Man Could Smell Like"—in order to market library services, anything from laptops to snack zones, to their students. The video went viral and has accumulated millions of views in just a few years. The message? If you want better grades, use the library.

The library as a key to success is a common message—find a needed book, an available computer, answers to questions, and all in one convenient place that is free to the public. It is such a great message that libraries are constantly exploring new ways to communicate it. While video production was clunky and cost prohibitive in the past, the digital revolution has made video an affordable and highly attractive marketing medium for today's library. Platforms such as YouTube have made the distribution of video content cheaper and easier than ever.

Your library can use video to share its stories and messages with the public. This chapter discusses the benefits of video-sharing sites, using video as a marketing tool, the video creation process, and how to publish, promote, and assess video content in order to provide an understanding of the medium for libraries looking to be seen and heard.

ONLINE VIDEO STREAMING

This section examines video sharing sites, emphasizing the two most popular: Vimeo and YouTube.

Video Sharing Sites

Online video sharing is now ubiquitous. It is almost difficult to believe that the first YouTube video was uploaded on April 23, 2005 (Schroeder 2010). Video is an integral part of the social media matrix and the web especially through the copy-and-paste convenience of embedded code. Even if your library never creates videos, you likely share them using Facebook, Google+, or other networking sites.

Video-sharing sites such as YouTube and Vimeo are logical tools for the storage and delivery of video content. Video files are significantly larger than image or audio files and can quickly consume valuable server space, which makes local file hosting cost prohibitive. YouTube and Vimeo provide storage, a compatible media player, and a social media framework at little or no cost. Both services are user-friendly and provide step-by-step instructions for how to set up accounts.

Even if your library is unable to make its own videos, you can still participate in online video communities through sharing. Try establishing a channel on YouTube and creating playlists of videos on relevant topics. For example, if your summer reading program selects *Eat, Pray, Love* to read, your library could build playlists of videos about the three locations Elizabeth Gilbert discusses in her book.

Your channel can also aggregate new videos from other channels that are of interest to your patrons. YouTube publishes them in a feed that displays much like the wall on Facebook. However, instead of just fans and likes, YouTube success measures include subscriptions, likes, comments, and favorites. When your channel likes or favorites a video from another channel or subscribes to a new channel, it displays on your feed. Libraries control the feed through the account settings under "Tabs." Using video-sharing sites, even without creating content, is a great way to complement your other marketing efforts.

YouTube versus Vimeo

The two largest and most well-known video-sharing sites are YouTube and Vimeo. YouTube was created in 2005 and was purchased by Google in 2007. With billions of reported views per month, YouTube is unquestionably the largest video hosting site in the world. YouTube accounts are free, as is their video hosting service (Power 2011). A basic YouTube account allows for video uploads longer than fifteen minutes once the option to increase your limit has been selected. If an uploaded video is subject to a copyright claim or strike, your account will reset to the fifteen-minute limit. Older YouTube restrictions on time and storage space no longer exist. For the most current account provisions, visit YouTube's "Help" section (http://support.google.com/youtube/).

Vimeo is a smaller operation with only millions of views per month. There is a free account option, which limits the number and size of uploads per week. There are Plus and Pro accounts that expand not only upload limits but also site usability and analytics. The biggest advantage of Vimeo over YouTube is video quality (Powers 2011). While YouTube compresses uploaded video content, Vimeo maintains the original file size. Vimeo also allows added customization, such as the ability to upload what displays in the video placeholder frame, a wider range of copyrighting options, and custom URLs.

Both YouTube and Vimeo provide statistical data on views, shares, and comments. Vimeo reserves their more robust statistical tools for Plus and Pro users, but you can still see your views over a timeline with the basic free account. Analytics are an important part of using video-sharing sites that will be discussed later in the chapter.

Uploading videos to both services has become easier in the last several years. Many video editors, such as MovieMaker, iMovie, and Camtasia, have a built-in upload function that routes your video directly to the popular video sharing site of your choice. There is no right or wrong choice when it comes to selecting a video sharing site for your library—both YouTube and Vimeo are excellent platforms for hosting and sharing videos.

53

MARKETING WITH VIDEO

Video sharing sites differ from other social media platforms in that, instead of largely reusing or sharing content, they promote content created at the local level. Marketing videos in particular are most effective when tailored to a target audience. Libraries can use video to market services, collections, spaces, events, and much more. Examples of common categories of marketing videos include marketing services, marketing collections, marketing spaces, and marketing events.

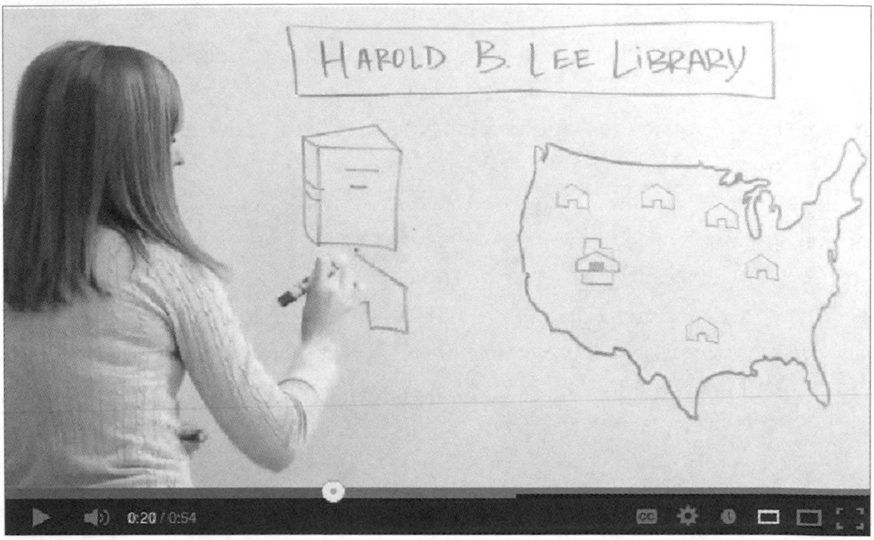

FIGURE 4.1
"Interlibrary Loan," a YouTube video by Harold B. Lee Library

Marketing Services

A great example of marketing a library service is the video "Interlibrary Loan Whiteboard" (www.youtube.com/watch?v=89eetuA5xP8), also produced by HBLL, shown in figure 4.1. It is short, to the point, and visually engaging, and explains the many advantages of using ILL. When creating a video to market services, resist the urge to discuss every aspect of a service and how it works. If your intention is to create a video that shows patrons how a service works, create an instructional video. If you want to promote the service so its usage increases, create a marketing video. If you want to both market and instruct: create two videos that can interlink on your channel. Do not create a video that attempts to do both at the same time or your messages will be confusing, and the potential impact will diminish.

Marketing Collections

Libraries are full of the rare and marvelous collections that can benefit from video treatment. A good example is the video "Monster Ball: The 2012 Anti-Prom" from the New York Public Library (http://youtu.be/UlYUUSFHbFE), which not only showcases three different collections but also shows patrons interacting with them and using the materials to create new content of their own. The visit to the library

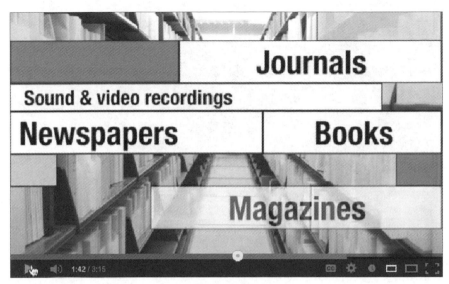

FIGURE 4.2
"Library Orientation," a YouTube video by University of Houston Libraries

is a component of a larger project; thus, the video is part of a larger playlist that involves community partners. Bringing in patrons and collaborating with other organizations are just two ways to market your collections to a wider audience.

Marketing Spaces

One of the most popular video types in librarianship is the orientation or virtual tour. This can be especially useful if your library reorganizes or augments its space or if your patron base is subject to regular turnover, such as school or university libraries. The University of Houston Libraries created an orientation video (www.youtube.com/watch?v=r0R_83Ykr8s) to promote the libraries' services and resources during the first weeks of school, as shown in figure 4.2, and LibGuides for freshman and sophomore level classes. The video introduces the library system's physical and online spaces, collections, and services.

Marketing Events

Libraries host any number of events, celebrations, or observances that can benefit from video promotion. You can tape footage from an event one year and then use it to promote the same event in the future. You can also create retrospectives of

FIGURE 4.3
YouTube video for Duke University's 2010 Edible Book Festival

events to share and thus extend your user base. Duke University Libraries host an annual Edible Book Festival; their promotional videos showcase entries in order to whet the appetite of prospective participants and attendees (fig. 4.3).

VIDEO CREATION PROCESS

The video creation process includes a variety of different steps as shown below. Best practices are included in the steps.

Getting Started

Video is a medium that gets people excited. Unfortunately, enthusiasm for the method can sometimes obscure a vital truth—not every marketing message is best communicated using video. The very first step in the video production process is deciding whether or not to make a video at all. Below are three questions you should ask yourself in order to test the feasibility of your video idea:

1. Is it already a movie in your mind? If you are not able to see the video in your mind, your concept is probably not best communicated using a

series of images. A single sheet flyer or a series of Facebook posts may be equally or even more effective.

2. Is the movie attainable? If your visualization involves a lengthy animation sequence that you cannot possibly reproduce, consider exploring other options. Or if your video hinges on securing the participation of local celebrities or rights to copyrighted materials, the cost and time involved may outweigh the benefits. You should always consider the cost effectiveness of the video creation process. Although the tools are relatively inexpensive, your greatest cost will be in staff time. For your first video, expect to spend as much as ten hours in production per minute of completed footage. Weigh all the advantages and disadvantages of creating a video before committing to the process.

3. Is the movie legal? If you plan to parody or imitate the work of another creator but cannot do so without violating copyright, then you should not proceed. YouTube will flag your video as containing stolen content, which can lead to legal action. Unless you can produce an original imitation, such as the one from HBLL, it is best to stay out of the parody game.

Once you are ready to start creating a video, get organized. The video development and creation process is lengthy and complex because it entails bringing a wide range of resources (e.g., images, video, audio, text) into a single container. Before you start to write a script, shoot video, or take pictures for your video, create a file folder on your computer for storing the component parts of your video. Name the folder with the title of your video, and create subfolders for documents (e.g., script, storyboard), images, video, and audio. Now you are ready to start writing content and gathering materials.

Creating the Video

There are several key elements to remember when developing a video for marketing purposes:

> **Keep your video short.** Advertisements are typically short as are most You-Tube videos. Wistia, a video-hosting service that works with businesses, released the following data in 2011 after analyzing viewership of their media library (Savage 2011). They found that viewership progressively

declined the longer a video played. The report concluded that videos should be short and direct and that the most important information should be communicated in the first twenty seconds when viewers are most engaged. This ensures that even if viewers do not watch all of your video, they will walk away with the most necessary information. Instruction videos can be longer than marketing videos, because the viewer has a vested interest in the end results—for example, learning all the steps of a process. But a marketing video is, in essence, a commercial: keep it short with a clear takeaway message.

Keep your message simple. The HBLL video's message is memorable because the message is clearly stated and concise: the library will help you get better grades. There is often a temptation to use video to communicate many messages all at the same time. Although a video blends audio and visual media, it does not mean the video should multitask when it comes to delivering the message. Once you have an idea for a video, such as making a video about an audiobook collection, write a purpose statement for the video. In other words, write the task you think the video should accomplish; for instance, "The purpose of this video is to increase usage of the audiobook collection."

Write objectives. Once you have a purpose, write objectives, or steps, for how you will accomplish the purpose. For example, if you are creating a video to promote your library's audiobook collection, one objective might be that patrons will learn where the audiobooks are located in the library. Ensure that the objectives are balanced against the length and purpose of your video. A less-effective objective for the audiobook video might be: "Patrons will learn how to download library audiobooks onto their mobile devices." While this objective is related to the purpose, it will consume a large amount of screen time. A better objective would be: "Patrons will learn that they can download library audiobooks to their mobile devices." This is a great selling point for any library audiobook collection and will also be easy to communicate with minimal screen time. Another video could be developed to show how to download the books. Keep your list of objectives short—three to five is usually enough. If you have more than five objectives, you may want to consider making more than one video to cover your topic. Gilchrist and Zald's chapter on "Instruction and Program Design through Assessment" (2008) discusses how to write learning outcomes, and is an excellent resource for understanding the structure and purpose of measurable objectives. Try reverse-writing objectives for some of your favorite TV commercials and see what patterns emerge that you can apply to your own advertisement as practice.

Write a script. Once you have established your video's purpose and objectives, it is time to write a script. Using your objectives as an outline, list all the images or actions required to achieve each objective. For the sample objective "Patrons will learn that they can download library audiobooks to their mobile devices," you will need an image of the download link, an image of compatible mobile devices, and perhaps pictures of incompatible mobile devices. Write a concise explanation of how it works: "You can even download select audiobooks directly from the library's catalog onto many phones and tablets. Currently, this service is not available for Android phones." There are a few writing practices that are important for producing a good script. First, remember that your script will be heard, not read. Use natural language and a conversational style. Beware of using library jargon. The best way to avoid using confusing jargon is to have a friend or patron read your script and identify any terms or concepts that they find confusing. While colleagues are also valuable editors for your script, a friend will be more likely to tell you they have no idea what "link resolver" means.

Gather materials. This chapter is not long enough to discuss how to capture live video and/or screencasts and how to record audio. There are numerous screencast programs (including freeware, open source, and proprietary), and a quick search for the best screencast software for your operating system will provide you with a current overview of features and usability. Use Audacity, available from SourceForge, to record audio. It is a well-established, free-to-download audio editor and is also relatively easy to use. You can use Audacity to trim out mistakes and dead space, and to add effects, such as fade-ins and fade-outs. Do not use a headset or other cheap microphones to record audio. Poor audio will immediately decrease the professional quality of your video and is a problem that can be averted by investing in a USB microphone (approximately $75 at the time of this writing).

FIGURE 4.4

Sample storyboard page for an Audiobook Collection promotional video

Create a storyboard. The next step is to create a storyboard. Use presentation software, such as Microsoft PowerPoint or Apple Keynote, to storyboard your video. Use the slides to place and organize any visuals (e.g., symbols, still photographs, video) and use the notes field for your script. The storyboard need not be polished or presentable. In fact, your storyboard is more likely to resemble an in-process scrapbook page, as shown in figure 4.4.

Assemble your video. PowerPoint and Keynote both have a built-in feature for exporting files as movies, but they lack an important editing feature for video creation: audio manipulation. While a soundtrack can be added to a presentation file, you must accept the audio file's length, volume, and sound quality and you will only be able to manipulate the slides in order to line up audio with selected video segments. A video editor is required to manipulate both audio and video to create an integrated production. There are several affordable or free video editors that will suffice for assembling basic images, video, and audio into a polished production. Windows MovieMaker is available as a free download to Windows users. Apple's iMovie is part of their iLife suite and is preinstalled on any Macintosh computer. Video editors are often built around a drag-and-drop functionality that allows you to grab images, video, and audio and to place them in a timeline. Both MovieMaker and iMovie have a media browser built into the editing interface to enhance this functionality. For example, you can browse your iTunes library from the comfort of the iMovie window, which allows you to preview the audio and then drag a selected file from the media browser into the project area, instead of having to open a separate screen, search for a file, and then import it.

Edit the video. Editing is where you fine-tune the component parts of your video into a cohesive whole. Some of the more important tasks you can complete using a video editor are:

Shortening and lengthening clips. Most video editors drop all images into your project timeline at a standard length. However, you may want one image to be five seconds long, while the next image need only be three seconds long. You may need to trim video clips to include only the most relevant portions. Shortening and lengthening video and audio is essential to establishing the pace of your video. If your video is too slow or too fast, reexamine how long it takes for everything to happen and make adjustments.

Changing the speed of a video clip. This is especially useful when working with screencast footage. As an example, if you are a slow typist, you can use your video editor to hasten your performance at the keyboard in the video clip. You can also create a time lapse effect by speeding up video footage. For instance, you can record people entering and exiting the library over a period of time and then speed up the footage to emphasize your facility's level of activity.

Adding text. Use the video editor to add text identifying the speaker if your video includes an interview or talking head. You can also use the "Add Text" feature to create credits for your video. Text may also be used to create effects such as equipment "talking."

Synchronizing audio with video. Line up the audio with your video and images. You can also add fade-ins and fade-outs, raise or lower audio in relation to other tracks (referred to as ducking), or raise the project's volume without creating ugly feedback or spiking, called normalization.

61

Adding transitions. Include fades, blurs, page turns, and other effects that can smooth movement from one clip to the next. Do not use transitions to the point where they become a distraction.

Branding your video. A brand does not need to display from the first moment of a video to the very last, but make sure you at least briefly place your logo at the beginning and the end.

Good editing takes time. Do not rush the process or expect that your first attempt to assemble content will be your last. An excellent test of whether or not your editing process has been thorough and successful is if, when asked, you can explain the various choices made in assembling the content. Thus, it will be clear that your editing decisions are not arbitrary and are necessary to the construction of a fluid narrative.

PUBLICATION, PROMOTION, AND ASSESSMENT

Once you have the video recorded with sounds and effects, there is still some work required to have it found and used effectively. The steps below will help guide you through the process:

Prescreen. Video editing is an arduous process. Similar to writing a lengthy document, it becomes difficult to be an objective, observant editor after hours of work. Prescreen your video for several work colleagues to assure quality and accuracy. Once you have prescreened the video for coworkers, prescreen it with several members of your target audience. As mentioned before, have them identify any terms they do not understand. Prepare a feedback form that checks for comprehension of your video's message and for the clarity of its presentation.

Publish. YouTube and Vimeo both provide privacy settings that are important to know about when publishing your video. There are three basic privacy settings available on YouTube: private, unlisted, and public. A user must be logged into the channel account to see videos set to private. Unlisted videos can be seen by anyone with a link to the video. Use the unlisted setting for any prescreenings of your video, or to make a video available only to a particular audience. Public videos are, of course, available to anyone. Vimeo's privacy model is more granular and is closely tied to its user communities; for example, you can post a video that only your subscribers can see. You can also post a video that is password protected. You can, at any time, change the privacy settings of a video on either Vimeo or YouTube.

Copyright. YouTube offers two standard methods of copyrighting videos: the standard YouTube license and a Creative Commons Attribution license which allows reuse of content. Vimeo offers the full spectrum of Creative Commons licenses. It is a good idea to involve your library's administration in the selection of an appropriate level of copyright protection for library-produced videos. If your video involves noninstitutional creative talents—such as outside musicians, narrators, photographers, or videographers—even if the people volunteer their services, your library should secure a creative content release. It is always best to be conscientious when it comes to copyright, and tools such as Creative Commons make it easy to share and protect content responsibly.

63

Upload. As mentioned earlier, most video editors have built-in menu options that will upload your video directly into popular video sharing sites. If using YouTube, be mindful that once you upload a video, you will not be able to update or swap it. If a video requires an update (for example, your catalog is updated and all your screen captures are of the old interface), you will need to upload the new video alongside the old copy. You can either make the old version inactive by changing its privacy settings to unlisted or private or you can delete the old video. If you delete a video, be certain to download and save all statistics first.

Describe and tag. Use descriptors or tags to catalog your video and make it more discoverable. At the University of Houston, we tag all our videos with *UH*, since students are more likely to use this abbreviation to find our channel than to type out three complete words. Create a set of standard tags that are attached to every video your organization produces. This will help connect your videos on the site, especially when YouTube searches for videos to populate the suggestions that display at the end of a viewed video.

Caption. YouTube has an auto-caption tool. There is also a third-party application called CaptionTube that you can use to program closed-captioning for your video. Closed-captioning of videos is essential to ensure compliance with ADA regulations. Captions also allow for your video to play where speakers or headphones are not available—such as in a quiet space of the library—and still be helpful to patrons.

Promote. The promotion of your video is ultimately all about placement. Your audience has to be able to find the video in order to view it. You can easily integrate your video into other social media platforms, such as Facebook or Google+, in addition to YouTube and Vimeo. If your library uses blogs, embed your videos into a post. Thousands of libraries use LibGuides, and their media embedding tool makes it easy to add videos. Strategic placement is more powerful and easier to assess than blanket dispersal. For example, if you develop a video about how to find a book on the shelf, placing the video on Facebook is not going to be as effective as placing it on a call number guide or placing a QR code for the video on the boxes of scrap paper in your library that patrons use to write

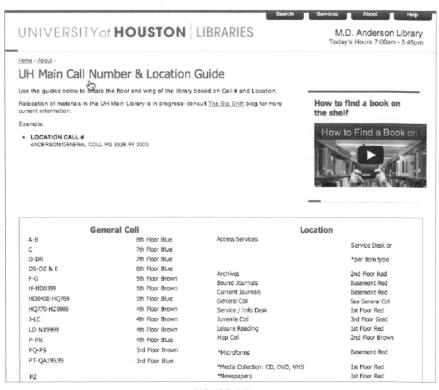

FIGURE 4.5
Call Number & Location Guide, University of Houston Main Library

down call numbers. When prescreening the video, ask your target audience where they would expect to find your video and they may provide additional strategic locations for video placement. An example of good placement is shown in figure 4.5.

Remember that although your video is being hosted on YouTube or another source, the vast majority of users will find your video somewhere else. In fact, you will be able to use the analytics on the video sharing site of your choice to see exactly how users find and view your video.

EVALUATING, ASSESSING, AND USING STATISTICS

Assessment is essential to the video production process. Assessment is more than tallying up the number of views a video receives—it is about measuring the effectiveness of the video's message, packaging, and placement. Analytics can tell you a great deal about your video and its effectiveness.

YouTube analytics break out statistics into several different categories, including views, demographics, playback locations, traffic sources, and audience retention. Demographics and views tell you a little about your viewers, including their geographical location, gender, and age group.

Traffic sources and playback locations are particularly important. These analytics tell you how people find and watch your video. Under "Playback Locations," you can see how people watch your video, whether it is an embedded form of your video, on a mobile device, directly via YouTube, or other methods. You can also see more specifically where people are finding your video under "Traffic Sources," including the domain name where the video was accessed, which search terms led people to your video, and whether your video was recommended by YouTube, Google, or another site. Traffic sources will sometimes confirm what you already know, but more often will surprise you. For instance, you may find that your video is being borrowed by another organization or that it is primarily being watched on your website and not on your social media platforms.

Once your video reaches a certain threshold of views, YouTube provides audience retention meters that track viewership across the timeline of your video. This can help you identify drop-off points, or spots where viewers stop watching your video. The viewing meter also reveals places where viewers rewind and re-watch footage, which is helpful to know when thinking about developing additional videos. There are two attention meters: absolute views (which are unique to your video) and relative views (which are compared against the average audience retention for YouTube's entire video catalog).

Examine all the available metrics before drawing any conclusions when evaluating video statistics. The most powerful data will come from evaluating usage using more than one metric. For example, your video may only result in a hundred views—but if users are watching it from beginning to end, you can assume that your video is important to at least those hundred viewers and should remain active. As with any marketing tool and strategy, it is important to know your users and meet their particular needs.

BEST PRACTICES AND CONCLUSIONS

The question remains: why use video to market libraries? Video is a narrative tool as well as visual, both of which are attractive characteristics to many people. Thus, it is a strong marketing tool for libraries and nonprofit organizations in general if done correctly. Be sure to use a short and memorable message. Follow the best practices discussed in the chapter. Video communicates stories to a broad audience, and libraries have amazing stories to share about their purpose and value. While the creation process is time intensive, it is more affordable than ever before to produce a video. Visual media continue to serve as marvelous avenues of creativity and ideal platforms for communication—in other words, the perfect marketing mixture.

REFERENCES

Gilchrist, Debra, and Anne Zald. 2008. "Instruction and Program Design through Assessment." In *Information Literary Instruction Handbook*, edited by Christopher N. Cox and Elizabeth Blakesley Lindsay, 164–192. Chicago: Association of College and Research Libraries.

Power, Don. 2011. "YouTube vs. Vimeo: Which Video Site Is Better for Business?" *Sprout Insights* (blog). August 31. http://sproutsocial.com/insights/2011/08/youtube-vs -vimeo-business/.

Savage, Chris. 2011. "4 Ways to Keep Viewers Engaged in an Online Video." Wista.com blog. February 7. http://wistia.com/blog/4-ways-to-keep-viewers-engaged-in -an-online-video/.

Schroeder, Stan. 2010. "YouTube's First Video Uploaded Five Years Ago Today." Mashable. April 22. http://mashable.com/2010/04/23/first-video-youtube/.

Outreach and Marketing Using Pinterest

Shae Martinez, Texas Health Presbyterian Hospital Dallas, Medical Library

Joyce McFadden, Baylor Health Sciences Library

PINTEREST: A NEW TOOL

Social networking sites have become a major component of advertising services, resources, and events, and a useful tool for staying connected with patrons. As library budgets shrink, technology advances, and users spend more time on sites such as Twitter and Facebook, libraries have found it useful—even necessary—to find ways to use these sites as platforms, not only for delivering information but also for obtaining useful feedback from—and gauging the interests of the communities they serve (Notess 2012a). Currently, meeting their users where they live has meant that libraries need to be online. Facebook and Twitter are good places for libraries to establish themselves because they have the largest market share of users compared to other social networking sites today (Notess 2012a). Lately, however, another major player has made its way onto many libraries' radars: Pinterest.

Pinterest launched in 2010 and immediately experienced rapid growth (Delo 2012). During its beta phase, Pinterest grew faster than Facebook and Twitter. In March 2012, Pinterest became the third largest social network in the world (Messner 2012). Pinterest represents a unique new tool for social media users. Described as a "virtual pinboard," Pinterest is a bookmark managing site that gives its users a space to collect, organize, label, and share things, such as images and linked video stills that they find online. Items that are added are called pins (Ekart 2012; Pinterest 2012). Pinterest was created specifically for sharing information visually; thus it allows for more functionality in this regard than either Facebook or Twitter

(Thornton 2012). Pinterest users, often called pinners, create boards. Boards are collections for groups of pins that pinners upload, capture from the Internet, or repin from other pinners, around themes and subjects of interest. These boards can be arranged, named, and organized in any way that a pinner chooses. Pins can be given descriptions, liked, and linked. Pinners can follow other pinners' boards, and like and repin other pinners' pins. Additionally, Pinterest can be used in conjunction with Facebook and Twitter; Pinterest accounts can be created using already existing Twitter and Facebook accounts. A Pinterest app is also available via Facebook that makes it possible for a Pinterest tab to be added to a Facebook page. A library can set up simultaneous sharing between accounts by starting a Pinterest account with an existing Facebook or Twitter page or by adding the Pinterest tab to a Facebook page.

While most pinners use Pinterest recreationally for things such as planning events and collecting and sharing recipes, retailers are increasingly turning to Pinterest as a tool to attract business. Pins linked to retailer sites help bring traffic to online stores in a fun way (Thornton 2012). Searches made on the Pinterest main site indicate that plenty of libraries are interested in using Pinterest to the same end. As an important note, Pinterest does not provide user data to publishers or commercial groups (Vega 2012).

In this chapter, we discuss the creation and maintenance of a Pinterest account and explore the potential of Pinterest as a marketing tool for libraries. Examples of well-designed Pinterest sites are included.

ESTABLISHING AN ACCOUNT

Similar to some other social media sites, early in its development Pinterest required that users receive or request an invitation to create an account during its beta phase. Now users can visit Pinterest to register for an account using an e-mail address or an existing Twitter or Facebook account. The next section provides instructions for creating a Pinterest account for your library. The first section of the instructions discusses creating a Pinterest account using an e-mail address. The next section describes the steps required to add a Pinterest tab to a library's Facebook page.

Creating a Pinterest Account Using an E-mail Address

It is strongly recommended that an institutional e-mail address be used instead of an employee's personal or work e-mail address. The institution thus retains control

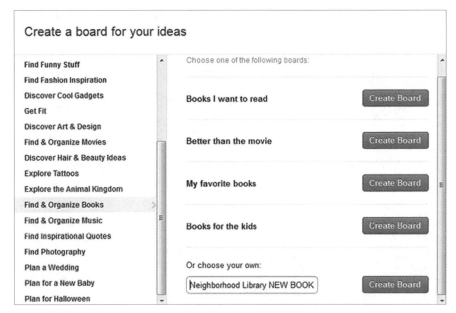

FIGURE 5.1
Creating a Pinterest board

of the site regardless of staff turnover issues. From the main Pinterest site (http://pinterest.com), click the "Sign up with Your E-mail Address" link to get to the creation screen. Your user name will become the last part of your Pinterest page's URL; for example, http://pinterest.com/neighborlib.

Upload a photo for your library's Pinterest page and fill in the "Create Your Account" screen with your library's information. Because your user name will also be part of your page's URL, it is best to use the same user name as your other social media sites for the sake of consistency (Ekart 2012). Once you submit this information, your library's Pinterest page will be complete. You will be directed to an orientation page and given options to help you create your first Pinterest board based on your interests, as shown in figure 5.1. Consider this a beginning exercise and follow it through. You can start by creating a board you already have planned or delete the test board later. We chose "Find & Organize Books" from the options and were presented with different board options, as well as given the opportunity to create and name our first board ourselves. We discuss populating Pinterest boards in the next section of this guide.

Pinterest page settings can be changed at any time by clicking on "Settings" under the menu in the top right-hand corner of your Pinterest page. The menu will be headed with your library's name—specifically, whatever portion of the library's name that was entered into the "First Name" field during the account registration process.

Linking a Facebook Page and Pinterest Account

The Pinterest tab used in these instructions represents one of many options available through Facebook. The instructions are intended for use by those who have Facebook profiles and who have also been added as an administrator for the library's Facebook page. Log in to Facebook and go to your library's Facebook page. Type *Pinterest* in the search box at the top of the page. Scroll down and select "Pinterest Page App" under "Apps," as shown in figure 5.2. On the next page, select "Continue As Yourself." In the "Add Page Tab" window, click the "Choose Facebook Pages" drop-down menu and select your library's page.

On the next page, click the button to "Authorize the Tab Application," and then on the next page, click the drop-down menu to change the settings and make your posts "Public" as shown in figure 5.3. Click the "Go to App" button. Enter your Pinterest account user name into the "Pinterest Username" field in your library's Facebook page "Pinterest Tab Settings" registration screen. In our example, we entered *neighborlib* as our user name during the Pinterest account registration process; thus, we entered *neighborlib* in the "Pinterest Tab Settings" field. Click the "Save Settings" button. A Pinterest tab will now be visible from your library's Facebook page. Visitors to your Facebook page will be able to see your pinboards via your Facebook page by clicking on the Pinterest tab.

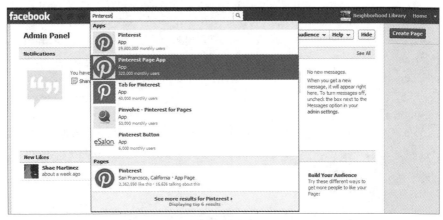

FIGURE 5.2
Connecting Pinterest and Facebook

Using the Pinterest Page App in conjunction with your library's Facebook page will allow you to share your pins on your library's Facebook page once you pin them to your Pinterest pin boards using the "Pin It" button. After pinning an image to one of your boards from another website using the "Pin It" button, Pinterest will present you with a dialogue window asking if you would like to "See your Pin," "Tweet your Pin," or "Share on Facebook."

To simultaneously share your pin on your library's Facebook page, click the "Share on Facebook" button. If you have not already logged in to your Facebook page, you will be prompted to do so. On the next window, click on the "Share" drop-down menu and select "On Your Page". Another drop-down menu will appear under that menu. Select your library's page, add any text that you would like to accompany the posted pin, and then click the "Share Link" button. As indicated in figure 5.4, the pin will appear as a shared link on your library's Facebook wall.

New pins added to your library's Pinterest boards also appear under the Pinterest tab on your library's Facebook page. It is always best to verify that the pins showing under the Pinterest tab on your library's Facebook page match the pins pinned to your library's actual Pinterest page.

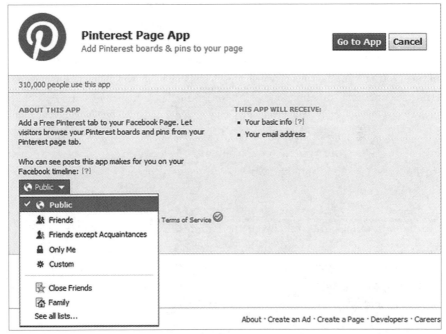

FIGURE 5.3
Pinterest tab settings

FIGURE 5.4
Sharing a pin on a Facebook page

Testing during the writing of this chapter indicated that you may not always be able to see your library's Pinterest tab when you are using Facebook as your library rather than as yourself. However, we found a solution for this that seems to work consistently. If, while signed into Facebook and using Facebook as your library, you are unable to see your library's Pinterest boards after clicking on the tab, click the drop-down arrow at the top right-hand corner of your Facebook page and switch between accounts so that you are using Facebook as yourself. Search for your library's page in the Facebook search box and go to your library's Facebook page. Once you are on your library's Facebook page as yourself, click the Pinterest tab. You should now be able to see your library's Pinterest boards, as shown in figure 5.5.

Be sure to "Refresh Cache" each time you view your library's Pinterest boards via the Pinterest tab. Do this from inside the Pinterest Page App tab page by scrolling to the bottom of the page and clicking "Refresh Cache" in the bottom left-hand corner of the page. Refreshing the cache ensures that you are viewing the boards as they appear on your library's actual Pinterest page, with all the latest pins that have been added.

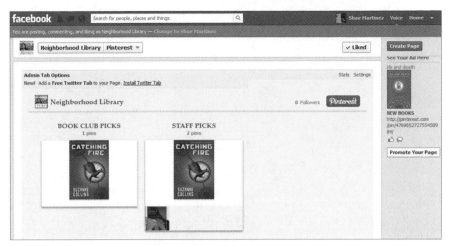

FIGURE 5.5
Sample Pinterest board for a library

POPULATING THE PAGE

Once your Pinterest page has been created, you may create boards and begin pinning. Simply put, a board is a "set of pins," and a pin is "an image added to Pinterest" (Pinterest/Getting Started 2012). There are two main ways to create boards for your Pinterest page. One way is by using the "+" button from the toolbar at the top of the main Pinterest page. After clicking this button, select "Create a Board," which allows you to name, categorize, and create your board. You may also create boards each time you upload, add, or repin pins. Each time a pin is added to a Pinterest board by uploading, adding, or repinning, Pinterest prompts the pinner to describe or add to the description of the pin and to categorize the pin by selecting the board to which it will be added. Click the drop-down menu in the pin window, above the description field, to see your boards or to add a new board.

There will be a drop-down menu when the "Create Pin" dialogue box opens. Click the drop-down menu arrow to see a list of your boards, along with the "Create New Board" option at the bottom of the list. Until you have at least four boards, Pinterest will give you the option to create boards directly from your main page by presenting you with empty boards. To build a board from one of these empty boards on your main page, simply click in the "Board Name" field, enter the name of your new board, and click "Create Board."

Pins may be added to your boards by uploading images from your computer or by adding images from other websites. There are two ways to add a pin from another website:

1. Click the "Add +" button from the toolbar at the top of the main Pinterest page, then click the "Add a Pin" button and enter the link of the page where the image you want to pin resides on the Internet.
2. Use the "Pin It" button to quickly and easily pin images from other websites onto your Pinterest page.

You may add the "Pin It" button to your browser by going to the "About" menu at the top right-hand corner of your Pinterest page and selecting the "Pin It" button. Instructions are provided by Pinterest on how to install the "Pin It" button into your browser, based on the browser you are using; for example, if you are using Internet Explorer when you begin installing the "Pin It" button, Pinterest will give instructions for installing the "Pin It" button into an Internet Explorer browser. Note that when you use the "Pin It" button to pin an image, the pin is automatically linked back to the page where you found it. According to Pinterest's site, this is to "credit the original creator" (Pinterest 2012). However, the links associated with a pin may be changed at any time by clicking the pin, and then clicking the "Edit" button.

You can also repin images from other pinners. Once you begin following other pinners on Pinterest, you will see their pins each time you log in to your library's Pinterest page. To find other pinners on Pinterest, use the search box at the top of the Pinterest page. By default, Pinterest searches for pins described with your search term. Once you enter your search terms in the Pinterest search box and clicking the magnifying glass, Pinterest returns a page of pins to match your search. Underneath the search box, you will see "Pins," "Boards," "Pinners"; click "Pinners" to see Pinterest users whose user names include your search terms. To repin an image from another pinner on Pinterest, hover your mouse over the pin and click the "Repin" button that appears over the pin. You will then have a chance to select the board on which you would like to pin the image, change its description, and pin it. You may also repin an image while viewing it in full size. To do this, click the pin; above the pin, to the left, you will see a "Repin" button. After clicking this button, choose the board on which you would like to pin the image, change its description, and pin it.

Pinterest describes a good pin as one that is pinned from an original source and pinned using a permalink. Users are encouraged to give credit to the creator of the pin and to include a "thoughtful" description (Pinterest 2012). Remember that when you pin images from other sites to your Pinterest board, they are linked back to the sites where you found them. Ekart (2012) suggests that libraries pin book images from their own online catalogs when possible, as these will be linked back to the catalog automatically. If a library's online catalog does not allow for this, Ekart (2012) suggests taking photos of books, then uploading the images, describing them, and pinning them with durable/permanent links to the library's catalog, as this process of taking and uploading their own images for pinning helps libraries avoid copyright issues. It also ensures that the link leads the user back to the library rather than to a vendor site. The link for a pin can be changed at any time by hovering over the pin, clicking the "Edit" button that appears, entering the desired address link into the "Link" field on the "Edit Pin" page, then clicking the "Save Pin" button.

There are some important things to know about copyright and Pinterest. Users have written articles about dismantling their Pinterest sites because of the copyright risks. Eder (2012) writes that "Pinterest, itself, is well-protected from lawsuits because of its policies and the Digital Millennium Copyright Act. But its users could be exposed to copyright suits by pinning content without a license, legal experts say. . . . The experts add that the best way to avoid problems is for Pinterest users to pin only content they create or have permission to use." A particular image might be pinned and repinned several times, making it very difficult to find the original site or even to give proper credit. Pinterest has actually created a NOPIN header tag for use by website owners who don't want their images pinned, and they have a method (http://pinterest.com/about/etiquette) by which users can notify them if a blatant copyright violation is found; however, the final responsibility still remains with the user.

What kinds of images can be pinned without risk, but still have promotional value? Ray (2012) presents a list of criteria that includes the following:

1. Use infographics (images that include graphics, text, and statistics)
2. Use e-books, guides, and white papers (specifically their cover images)
3. Display the library's work culture "behind the scenes"

MARKETING WITH PINTEREST

There are a variety of examples of marketing with Pinterest. For example, the American Physical Therapy Association (APTA) has a website with free downloadable patient care brochures that can be pinned. Messner (2012) and Notess (2012b) describe several other pin and board ideas for libraries: an illustrated guide to your library's classification system, book trailers (pinning book cover photos taken by the library), historical photos (owned by the library), visual resource guides, digital collection promotion, or collaborative gathering of images or promotion ideas. The Smiley Memorial Library at Central Methodist University (CMU) in Missouri uses Pinterest to create "research portals" and visual images of ideas to help students begin the research or writing process (Dudenhoffer 2012). The library also uses the site to manage recommendations for new books and to publish their new book lists. Users find the Pinterest boards much more interesting than simple text lists. Dudenhoffer (2012) notes the convenience of having a site that can be updated easily and quickly but that still retains the same URL. The library has built information literacy classes and an educational technology course using Pinterest. Even the potential copyright issues provide topics for discussion and education in crediting and citing from the Internet.

Other libraries are also beginning to find and explore ways to use Pinterest to advertise services, promote resources, and share news and information with their users. In an article about the use of Pinterest in academic libraries, Thornton (2012) discusses the Gordon Library of the Worchester Polytechnic Institute (http://pinterest.com/gordonlibrary) and its use of pinboards to showcase scans from items in their special collections as an "excellent model for virtually introducing . . . resources and information" using pinboards (Thornton 2012, 171). The pins link back to the Fellman Dickens Collections page on the library's website. Clicking on these pins automatically takes users to the library website, where they can read more about the Dickens Collection.

A search of Pinterest in October 2012 showed many more examples of how libraries are finding ways to use Pinterest. The Claude Moore Health Sciences Library (http://pinterest.com/claudemoorehsl) uses one of its boards for images of equipment that they own and lend; the board's description includes instructions for how to check out the equipment featured on the board (fig. 5.6). The Otis Library in Connecticut (http://pinterest.com/otislibraryct/) has several boards including a board with information about their Teen Summer Reading Program; a board featuring images of past library displays; and a board titled "On Our E-Readers," which, as its name suggests, holds images of e-books loaded onto e-book readers that are lent by the library (fig. 5.7). These pins are linked back to the library's online public catalog so interested, and eligible users can check their availability.

FIGURE 5.6
"Equipment the Library Owns" pinboard,
Claude Moore Health Sciences Library

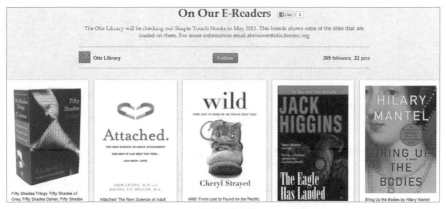

FIGURE 5.7
"On Our E-Readers" pinboard, Otis Library

MAINTAINING PINTEREST SITES

Maintenance of your library's Pinterest site will involve ongoing activity, and purposeful, well-planned pinning (Thornton 2012). Libraries may want to find other libraries to follow in order to find ideas for boards and for pins to repin. When you follow someone on Pinterest, you will see their pins in real time on Pinterest. You may either follow a pinner's individual boards, or you may follow all of a pinner's boards. Remember that you can "Unfollow" pinners or boards at any time, and that the pinner will not be notified.

You can follow all of a pinner's boards by clicking the "Follow All" button above that pinner's boards on the main Pinterest page or by clicking "Follow" under the pinner's profile picture returned in Pinterest pinner search results. From a pinner's

FIGURE 5.8
Following an individual Pinterest board

FIGURE 5.9
Pinterest pinboard as a virtual suggestion box,
Baylor Health Sciences Library

main page, click the "Follow" button on any one board to follow that board only (fig. 5.8).

Pins and boards may be edited at any time. There are two ways to edit a pin. To edit from the thumbnail view, hover your mouse over the pin, then click the "Edit" button that appears. To edit a pin from its full-size view, click the "Edit" button above the pin to the left of the screen. When editing a pin, you are given the options to delete the pin, change the board on which the board is pinned, change the source link for the pin, or change the description of the pin.

Because social networking is all about interaction, libraries may eventually want to allow other pinners to pin images to their boards. Some ideas for interactive library boards may be boards related to library-sponsored drawings or contests, or a perhaps virtual suggestion box, such as the one offered by the Baylor Health Sciences Library (http://pinterest.com/bhsl), which has a "Suggestions" pinboard where followers are invited to make suggestions (fig. 5.9).

Add contributors to a board by going to that board on your main Pinterest page and clicking the "Edit" button, or by going to the board and clicking the "Edit Board" button at the top of the page. From the edit page, you will see a "Who Can Pin?" field. Enter the names of pinners that you would like to add as contributors. Generally, you must follow a pinner in order to allow pinning rights on one of your pin boards. Furthermore, when you allow a pinner to contribute to one of your boards, that board will be visible on the contributor's Pinterest page in addition to your own.

BEST PRACTICES AND CONCLUSIONS

Trends in, and best practices for, the use of Pinterest by libraries are emerging. Based on the template provided by Pinterest during page creation, we recommend that libraries start their Pinterest pages with at least four boards. Libraries should try to start each of their boards with approximately ten pins (Ekart 2012). When possible, libraries should name their Pinterest pages just as they have named their other social networking accounts. As for other social media tools, libraries should connect their Pinterest pages with their websites, online catalogs, blogs, and other social networking accounts (Ekart 2012; Thornton 2012). Libraries should also be mindful of copyright law and use pin descriptions to give credit to outside sources as needed (Thornton 2012). The Pinterest page should be promoted through library signage as well as through other social media accounts and webpages (Ekart

2012). Lastly, libraries should stay active and add pins to their boards regularly (Thornton 2012). Thornton recommends designating a page administrator who sets aside time each week to add pins to the library's Pinterest boards (Thornton 2012).

REFERENCES

Delo, Cotton. 2012. "Pinterest". *Advertising Age* 83 (9): 32.

Dudenhoffer, Cynthia. 2012. "Pin It!" *College & Research Libraries News* 73 (6): 328–32.

Eder, Steve. 2012. "In Shift, Pinterest Says to Pin Your Own Stuff." *Wall Street Journal*, Eastern edition 259 (71): B6.

Ekart, Donna F. 2012. "Tech Tips for Every Librarian." *Computers in Libraries* 32 (5): 32–33.

Messner, Kate. 2012. "Very Pinteresting!" *School Library Journal* 58 (7): 24–27.

Notess, Greg R. 2012a. "Next Generation Social Networks and Search." *Online* 36 (3): 44–46.

Notess, Greg. R. 2012b. "Sharing to Multiple Social Networks." *Online* 36 (4): 45–47.

Pinterest. 2012. "Pinning 101." https://pinterest.com/about/help/.

Ray, Mitt. 2012. "7 Pinterest Tips for B2B Companies." *Social Media Examiner* (blog). June 20. www.socialmediaexaminer.com/b2b-pinterest-tips/.

Thornton, Elaine. 2012. "Is Your Academic Library Pinning? Academic Libraries and Pinterest." *Journal of Web Librarianship* 6 (3): 164–175.

Vega, Tanzina. 2012. "Marketers Find a Friend in Pinterest." *New York Times*. April 17. www.nytimes.com/2012/04/18/business/media/marketers-find-a-friend-in-pinterest.html.

Marketing Libraries with Google+

Amy West, University of Minnesota

Google+ is an attempt to leverage Google's massive user base into a coordinated identity service by using social features to knit together the existing Google product line. For example, Google Events connects the video chat service Hangouts with Google Calendar and Google Photos (formerly Picasa Web). Google+ now supports broadcast hangouts, communities (topical groups), organizes contacts into circles, sharing of Google Drive files, and photos and video from YouTube.

Google product users will find value from the integration of services they already use with the social features. Thus, for library users who already use Google, getting content from a library via Google+ will be a highly integrated experience that happens relatively seamlessly. Other social media content, such as Facebook updates, can also be more easily brought into Google+; for instance, through direct linking to the Google Calendar. Google+ is an asset for libraries using Google for their events calendars, user contacts, file creation and storage, photo storage and editing. Used well, Google+ can be a valuable tool for creating an integrated social presence.

Compared to other social media tools, Google+ is reasonably well designed. It connects Google's products, has good mobile applications, and already has a high number of potential users based on the use of Google Search. Specific features relevant to library marketing include:

> *Broadcast hangouts*—useful for author readings, instruction, and other activities

Communities—useful for book groups and other topical approaches

Contacts via Google+ Circles—target content via existing contacts

Google Drive files—can be shared, and include forms for assessing the services you provide to users

Events—useful to leverage Google Calendar and push events directly to Google Calendar

Photos—include photos with Google Events to create a single photo pool for an event, which can create a deeper sense of engagement

Google Search—helps ensure that your library comes up prominently in Google searches

When pursued rigorously, such as the New York Public Library's Google+ presence shown in figure 6.1, engagement levels seem, from the outside, to be on par with Facebook. However, there is "an unavoidable sense of emptiness in Google+" (Efrati 2012). Currently, there are few examples of libraries with active presences and engaged users in Google+. However, Google+ is not the ghost town some

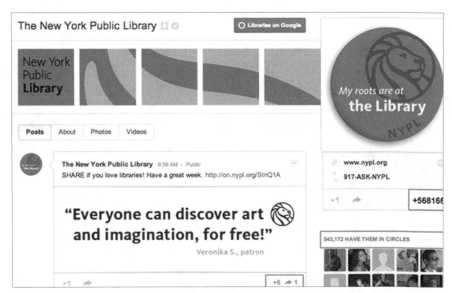

FIGURE 6.1
Google+ page for New York Public Library

people think it is, as it experienced a 66 percent increase in 2011 through 2012 (Bamburic 2012).

Working within the Google Apps environments can limit various features available to standard Google accounts. As an example, the author confirmed with her institution's IT staff that sharing files from Google Drive to Google+ is not available in the instance of Google Apps for Education used at the University of Minnesota. For the author, this significantly limits the value of Google+ as tool for communicating with her users. However, as more people and organizations explore Google+ as a social media tool, it is likely that most issues, including this one, will be remedied.

Google+ unfortunately requires that any institutional presence be tied to an individual. Thus, creating a Google+ page for a library is a task that must be tied to an individual. Although ownership of pages can be reassigned as needed, this is one more activity that must be monitored. Depending on the volatility of a library's staffing, this could progress into a maintenance issue. Including this task into a social media plan and regular procedures is vital.

Despite some flaws, a library that uses Google to provide a significant amount of its technology infrastructure—or whose patrons appear to be heavy users of Google+—may find Google+ to be an excellent choice for a marketing tool. However, if a library wants to reach the largest number of users on the most regular basis, Google+ may not be a good choice at this time, especially if it is the only social media tool. The New York Public Library presence, however, does demonstrate that there is an audience who uses Google+ and that it can be an effective marketing tool.

GOOGLE+ ACCOUNTS

Libraries have several options for establishing accounts. As mentioned above, there has to be a real person using her real or commonly accepted name already using Google+. Per the Google Names Policy, "Pages require a personal profile to act as the administrator of the page, though the administrator may remain anonymous to those interacting with the Google+ page" (Google 2011). Once one or more individuals have been designated to set up accounts, there are two relevant categories: pages and communities. Libraries do not have to have a page to create a community, although it is helpful.

The options for the types of pages include local businesses/places or institutions. Since the business/place option asks for a primary phone number immediately, this choice would work best for single-location libraries or branches within a larger system. Multiple location library systems should start with the institutional option.

Select a name for your library, indicate the users for which the content is appropriate, and agree to the "Google+ Pages Additional Terms of Service" (Google 2013). The current groups for determining appropriateness are everyone, two age groups, and "alcohol related". As with other social media tools, try to keep library names consistent and recognizable across marketing tools.

While the library staff managing the Google+ page should read and understand the additional terms of service (Google 2013), there are a few elements that warrant special attention:

1. With respect to the age groups, "Google reserves the right to restrict the content on your Google+ Page at its discretion."
2. With respect to content on pages, "Google reserves the right to block or remove Google+ Pages that violate . . . third party rights . . . "
3. "Google may, without notice, remove your Google+ Pages if they are dormant for more than nine months."

Libraries posting content about books may want to think through how they present content on pages because demands to ban books are, unfortunately, not rare. Unlike decisions about removing books from collections, the decision to remove a page is in Google's hands and not at the library's discretion.

Google has shown itself to be very interested in supporting third-party claims to intellectual property regardless of the merit of the claims. Recent attempts to remove a remix video consisting of content from *Buffy the Vampire Slayer* and the Twilight series demonstrate how little interest YouTube, which is owned by Google and tied to Google+, had in properly adjudicating an "entirely meritless copyright claim" (McIntosh 2013). A library might want to post video of author readings, clips from newly acquired resources, and similar items. Google's approach thus far has been to lock out any user whom it feels is acting against its terms of service, names policy, or other rules; this means that a library could find itself unable to access its own account. This is a case where libraries could help Google understand copyright and fair use.

Once a library has set up a page, it should keep it active, as Google reserves the right to remove a page if it becomes dormant. The library could lose access to photos as well as posts in that case. However, keeping pages up to date is a necessity for any social media tool.

Once a page is live, the library has many options: posting, +1 (similar to liking on Facebook), commenting, resharing others' posts, adding to circles other users who have added the library page, starting a hangout, and hosting an event. If necessary, the option to block and ignore people is also available. A library could choose to set up a circle, which is a group of contacts, although for promotional purposes this seems to be a feature of little use unless the library chooses to maintain one circle of all the users it discovers. Libraries could also have circles for smaller groups, such as summer reading participants. The primary promotional value of circles is to push notifications to users. This will be discussed more in the section on advertising. Internally, circles could be useful for tracking content shared by other libraries. Thus, if a library system has an individual page for each branch, then placing the other branches into a single circle makes it easy to learn about and to share content across library branch pages.

Once a library has a page, the communities feature will also be of use. For example, a library-run book club would be an obvious candidate. Communities are similar to Google Groups: they are topical, may require permission to join, may be private, and can send notifications on new content. Figure 6.2 provides an example of a community for librarians, LibTecWomen.

The communities feature was just introduced in December of 2012 and thus has yet to become popular. Communities also highlight two related issues for Google. A post at GigaOm in March 2012 noted that perhaps the biggest problem with adoption of Google+ is that, as a late entrant to social networks, "Google needs Google+, but Google users do not" (Ingram 2012). Users likely to use a social network seem to have already settled into existing sites such as Facebook and Twitter, and there is no clear imperative yet for using Google+, other than easily integrated options.

There is some overlap in the Google+ services, which can be confusing. For example, Google Groups, Google's dedicated forum tool, offers nearly all the same features as Google+ Communities. Events can also be set up as just regular meetings on a public calendar. It's not obvious, based on a feature comparison, when a library needs to use one tool and when to use a different one. Thus, libraries will want to make some decisions about how to use Google+ most efficiently for the best effect for patrons. It seems that a library can get the most benefit from Google+ if the library works with it as much as possible. For example, it might be best to decide up front that once a Google+ presence is established, all future library events will be handled as events and not simply just as open meetings in Google Calendar. Likewise, your library might create only communities and move its groups to Google+ Communities. However, despite the fact that Google+ has

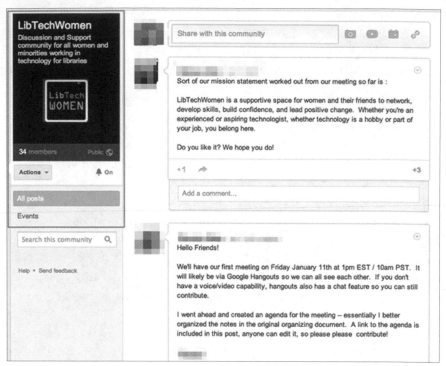

FIGURE 6.2
Google+ page for LibTech Women

been in operation since 2011, relatively slow adoption and periodic introduction of new features that overlap with existing products has made it difficult to find enough high-quality examples of library Google+ use to develop good practice guidelines that are unique to Google+.

All of that said, if the author worked in a library that was just beginning to establish a social presence, then Google pages and communities both appear to be effective methods for reaching out to library users. Pages bring with them the power of Google. Even Internet users who do not have Google accounts are likely to use Google Search. This means that unlike with Facebook pages—which are mostly gated within Facebook—current and potential users would see much more of a library's social presence through simple Google searches. Thus, setting up a solid Google+ presence can be a strong marketing tool.

FIGURE 6.3
Collection image, New York Public Library

POPULATING GOOGLE+

Libraries can populate the service with all the kinds of content available from networks such as Facebook and Twitter. For each section below that discusses specific Google+ features, the default setting should be "Public." Content on this setting is viewable to all Internet users who come across it, and it is sharable to other social networks.

Google+ posts can be either very short, such as Twitter tweets, or long, which might serve as a substitute for a separate blog. The NYPL typically includes an image illustrating each post they make, as demonstrated in figure 6.3. This is an excellent practice, as it keeps the page from being text heavy and gives the library the opportunity to show off visual materials from its collection. Libraries are encouraged to follow the NYPL's lead—and also to follow best practices for social media as discussed in this chapter, in other chapters of this book, and in other books and articles.

Photos

Photos are a formal section of Google+ and, name notwithstanding, also include videos in addition to photos. Photos are optimized for upload from mobile devices via instant upload, which is activated by default or from individual posts. Picasa, Google's desktop image editor, is well integrated with Google Photos. Google+ automatically creates an album of images added to posts, an album of profile pictures, and an album of instant uploads. Uploaded videos can come from or be sent to YouTube. A library may also choose to keep its videos uploaded only in Google+. However, as discussed in chapter 4, there is more opportunity for users to find your video content through connecting them to YouTube.

Google's requirement that content in Google+ be connected to individuals is a weakness with respect to the photos tool. While images uploaded via instant upload go to a private album, the connection of pages to individuals still leaves ample opportunity for accidental cross-posting. If library staff responsible for a library page also use Google+ for themselves, it will be important to make sure that the staff either turn off instant upload on their mobile devices or do not work on the library's page from their mobile devices. Picasa suffers from a similar problem: library photos edited in Picasa cannot be directly shared to a library page. Instead, they are uploaded to the account of the library staff person currently signed into Picasa. As mentioned before, with enough pressure, Google may consider allowing organizational accounts, just as Facebook made modifications to allow organizations to join.

Hangouts

Hangouts is the name Google+ uses for video conferencing. This is the best feature of Google+. One can hang out with groups of individuals, up to ten at once, or do a "Hangout On Air," known as a broadcast hangout, which would be ideal for author events where either bringing the author in to speak in person is not feasible or where a library covers a large geographic area and in-person attendance at events might be difficult. "Hangouts On Air" are automatically saved to YouTube, which permits library users to "attend" after the event is over. Hangouts are also great for meetings, although a library should be careful to change the default setting from

"Public" to whatever sharing level is appropriate (unless, of course, the meeting is public). Hangouts look like video conferences except that if a user comes across one that is ongoing, there will be an "on air" message.

Events

Events are another useful feature of Google+. Used to the fullest extent, an event brings together Google Calendar, Photos, and Hangouts, as shown in figure 6.4. Any individual or circle invited to an event will see the event on the calendar, and people joining an event, but not specifically invited, can add it to their own calendar. The event can be set as a hangout, and, if "Party Mode" is enabled, users of Android devices can upload images and video in real time. "Party Mode" should therefore be used with caution. Attendees of an event can also share their photos to a single album. This latter option is probably better for libraries. It encourages engagement without making it too easy for users to share content that might not be appropriate. The sharing of guest photos can be turned off in the "Actions" menu

89

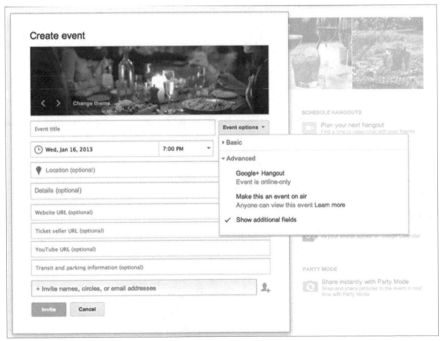

FIGURE 6.4
Google+ event setup

once an event has been created. Libraries may wish to use this option if they are concerned about unmoderated posting of photos and videos.

Google Drive Files

Google Drive files—particularly forms for service assessment and gauging user satisfaction with library services—can be shared via Google+ pages by making the file public and pasting the link into a post on a page. However, it is still not possible to share Google+ pages from inside of Google Drive. Using that path, the file will end up being shared on the staff person's Google+ stream and not on the library's page. This is another area where Google+ could be more cognizant of the need for changes to occur in order to allow organizations to use Google+ effectively.

MAINTAINING AND ADVERTISING

A benefit of using Google+ is that you can make your Google+ page eligible to show up on the right-hand side of the Google Search page for relevant queries, thus making your Google+ page more discoverable (Google 2013), as shown in figure 6.5.

In addition to this primary method of advertising, one use of Google+ Circles for library pages is to send notifications of new content to users. Unfortunately, the information displays differently depending upon the user's settings, and some users may turn notifications off completely. However, this is still a feature for libraries to try. Another more common advertising method is to use Google's AdWords service to direct traffic to the Google+ page.

The most effective way to promote a Google+ page is to regularly post interesting content with eye-catching visuals that addresses user needs. For example, if a library's users value knowing about new books that the library has acquired, a Google+ page would be an ideal location to highlight new acquisitions along with cover images. Ultimately, Google+ follows the rule for other social media: popularity depends on the user's perception of the usefulness of the information presented. People are likely to appreciate knowing about the upcoming events, newly acquired materials, and workshops a library offers. If a library's users already employ Google and find the library's Google+ page, the users can easily stay aware of the library's content.

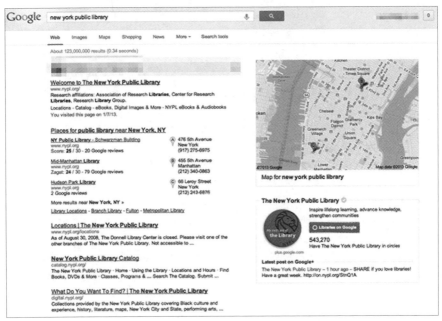

FIGURE 6.5
Google+ advertisement in Google Search

EVALUATING, ASSESSING, AND USING STATISTICS

At this point in Google+ development, it is not clear how a library would assess Google+ Pages effectively. Google+ does provide the number of +1s and reshares for each post, which offers some evaluative information. Libraries can probably assume that items that are liked and shared are useful and perhaps offer additional information on these topics. Items that are not shared or +1ed may need clarification, more user friendly terminology etc. According to the Google+ Help site, pages for businesses get usage statistics, but there is nothing specifically noted about pages for organizations. As Google+ enhances their services, one can hope that additional analytics become available, especially those that are useful for organizations.

If a library links its Google+ page to its main website, Google Analytics should provide some usage data. As well, if a post is publicly reshared, which occurs when a user sets the share to public when he reshares it, a library can use Google Ripples to see the effects. DiSilvestro (2012) describes Google Ripples and how to use Ripples for marketing. Libraries can explore these options to determine how best to use the data. As with all tools, regular assessment of users and responding to their comments is the best means of evaluation and assessment.

BEST PRACTICES AND CONCLUSIONS

The New York Public Library is as an excellent model of library use of Google+. The NYPL follows standard social media recommendations: they post regularly and in visually arresting ways, they mix content about events with posts on their collections, they include both basic library information (hours, directions) and events/specials, and they keep an informal but still professional tone in their posts. For the most part, the New York Public Library Google+ presence mirrors its Facebook presence and, to a lesser extent, its Twitter presence. Given the moderately high levels of +1s, moderate to low levels of reshares of their posts, but very high numbers of views, NYPL seems to have found a user group that values its Google+ presence. Libraries are advised to follow the NYPL example.

As mentioned, Google+ does have a significant weakness: it requires that all content, even content meant to represent institutions or businesses, be tied to specific people. This introduces opportunities for inadvertent cross-posting of content as well as significantly decreasing individual privacy by forcing the connection between an individual's personal and professional identities. Although Facebook also connects people and group content, Facebook isn't necessarily as popular as a search, e-mail, calendar, video, blogging, news-reading, and document storage tool. Google+'s potential lies in its ability to bring all these elements together.

Unfortunately, because Google+ requires that a single person be responsible for the page, this risks a single person's activities across both personal and professional domains be confused if she is doing so from her personal Google account. If a library and its staff members are all comfortable with this level of risk, Google+ can be very useful. Pages are easy to create and draw on the power of Google Search for promotion. Google+ ties into existing tools, including Google Calendar, Picasa Web, Chat, and Drive, thus making Google+ a potentially powerful tool for socially connected and tightly integrated content. The new Google+ Communities feature has great potential for library use, especially for book groups and similar events. Hangouts provide the opportunity for even small or isolated libraries to connect with authors virtually and to support other community events.

If Google+ continues to add improvements, especially those that solve some of the issues for organizations, Google+ will warrant a reexamination to see whether intervening changes make it a better option for libraries. Certainly, since its debut in 2011, it has improved significantly. One would hope that this record of steady service improvement will continue. If libraries, and other organizations, provide feedback to Google and Google+, it more likely that we will see the necessary improvements to make Google+ a highly useful social media tool.

REFERENCES

Bamburic, Mihaita. 2012. "Google+ and 'Ghost Town' Are a Contradiction." Betanews. July 27. http://betanews.com/2012/07/27/google-and-ghost-town-are-a-contradiction/.

DiSilvestro, Amanda. 2012. "Google+ Ripples Explained." *Search Engine Journal*. September 11. www.searchenginejournal.com/google-ripples-explained/48275/.

Efrati, A. 2012. "The Mounting Minuses at Google+." *Wall Street Journal*. February 28. http://online.wsj.com/article/SB10001424052970204653604577249341403742390. html.

Google. 2012. "Webmaster Tools: Google+ Pages." December 3. http://support.google .com/webmasters/bin/answer.py?hl=en&answer=1708844

Google. 2011. "Google+ Help: Google+ Profile Names Policy." Last updated 2013. http:// support.google.com/plus/bin/answer.py?hl=en&answer=1228271.

Google. 2013. "Google+ Policies & Principles: Google+ Pages Additional Terms of Service." Last updated 2013. www.google.com/intl/en/+/policy/pagesterm.html.

Ingram, M. 2012. "Google Plus: The Problem Isn't Design, It's a Lack of Demand." *GigaOM*. March 15. http://gigaom.com/2012/03/15/google-plus-the-problem-isnt -design-its-a-lack-of-demand/.

McIntosh, J. 2013. "Buffy vs Edward Remix Unfairly Removed by Lionsgate." RebelliousPixels blog. January 9. www.rebelliouspixels.com/2013/buffy-vs-edward -remix-unfairly-removed-by-lionsgate.

Foursquare: A New Marketing Tool

Anne Rauh, Syracuse University

Carolyn Rauber, University of Minnesota, Twin Cities

Foursquare is an application combining social networking, geolocation, and advertising. At its heart, Foursquare is a mobile app that encourages users to share their location recommendations with friends and provides an opportunity for businesses to offer incentives to current and potential customers.

Users can download the Foursquare app to their mobile device for free. Currently, Foursquare maintains apps on all major mobile platforms and also exists as a website. Because a user typically creates an account and "checks in" when he or she visits a location, Foursquare works best when a user's mobile device can be geolocated, either through global positioning systems (GPS) or Wi-Fi capabilities. A check-in on Foursquare lets others in the social network know you are at a physical location and provides further options.

The check-in is already a familiar concept for us. For instance, after checking in to a hotel, you might get local recommendations from the concierge. The Foursquare home page encourages user to check in. Similarly, Foursquare generates recommendations and provides deals and tips. As an added incentive, Foursquare assigns points to each check-in. With each check-in, users can see, scoreboard-style, the points they and their friends have accumulated over the course of a week.

Foursquare's "Explore" feature provides custom recommendations based on tips from other users, frequency of check-ins, and whether a user has indicated that they like a place. Foursquare might recommend a restaurant based on where your friends have checked in, whether a deal is available to Foursquare users, the popularity of the location, or how new the location is.

Businesses (and libraries) can get in on the game as well. A business manager starts by claiming the venues he manages. From there, he can post local updates, upload photographs, and post "specials." These activities enhance a venue's page and attract users.

Why should libraries use this tool? First of all, if your library is open to the public, there is a good chance that people are already checking in to your location via Foursquare. They do this in order to earn points and "badges," a Foursquare award for achieving certain goals, such as checking in to fifty locations. Libraries can also use Foursquare features, including specials and updates, to connect with their users. When a user checks in, he or she is automatically notified of the library's current specials and recent updates. Additionally, once you claim your library as a venue on Foursquare, you receive a weekly summary of activity, including the number of check-ins your library has received over the past week. Foursquare can serve as another way to view and assess how users interact with the library data.

In this chapter, we describe how to set up an account and claim your library as a venue, populate the outward-facing library venue page, use Foursquare for advertising, and evaluate Foursquare's impact. We highlight the New York Public Library as an exemplar of a Foursquare-engaged organization. The chapter concludes with a set of best practices and recommendations.

FOURSQUARE FOR MARKETING

As with other social media tools, there are a few steps needed to create an effective Foursquare page for marketing. The sections below guide you through the process.

Creating an Account

To implement Foursquare, a library must first create an account. Visit Foursquare's website, www.foursquare.com, and create an account with an email address and a password or sign up using an existing Facebook account. You can create a new account in the library's name or use your own personal account. It is best to create a general library account separate from any personal account, especially if you are already an active Foursquare user. This is particularly relevant if you plan to demonstrate Foursquare at a meeting or presentation—you might unintentionally show your colleagues where you checked in last weekend. You can assign additional administrators and transfer administrator duties at a later time. If you decide to create both a personal and a library account, make sure that you have a strategy for keeping them separate.

The first time you log in to Foursquare on the web, you will be given a list of suggestions. These suggestions might be people, brands, or institutions that you may wish to follow. You will also be asked if you would like to add Foursquare to your mobile device. Foursquare currently supports iPhone, Android, Blackberry, Windows Phones, WebOS, Symbian, Series 40, and Meego.

Once you have registered for Foursquare, take some time to use it before moving on to create your venue. If you have used it only on the web, try downloading the app on your mobile device. If you have never used Foursquare for recommendations, try the "Explore" button on your mobile device or use the web interface to explore venues nearby, as shown in figures 7.1 and 7.2.

Each time you visit a location that is represented on Foursquare, you are given the option to check in at those locations. When you check in, you are notifying other users that you are physically present in that location. Foursquare uses your mobile device's GPS to determine your location. Do not try to check in unless you are at that location as Foursquare attempts to prevent "cheating" by using GPS

FIGURE 7.1
"Explore Foursquare with Recommended Venues" screen

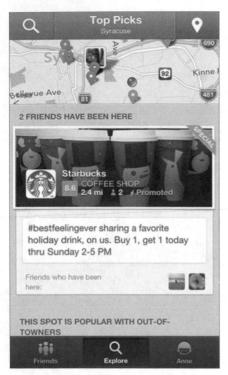

FIGURE 7.2
"Explore Nearby Locations with the Mobile App" Foursquare screen

to make sure that the position of your phone corresponds with your check-in location.

While exploring, you may see that, for each venue, Foursquare lists the total number of unique users who have checked in, the total number of times those users have checked in, and the number of people who are currently checked in at that venue. If you have connected with friends who use Foursquare, you will be able to see if any of your friends have visited that venue. In addition, you will see "mayors" listed for each venue. The "mayors" are the users who have checked in to that venue the greatest number of times in the past sixty days.

Once you have explored venues and connected with friends, you can begin checking in at venues and earning points. Points are awarded to Foursquare users for the different activities they perform. Some examples of activities that receive points are checking in, creating venues, becoming the mayor of a venue, and checking in with friends at a location together.

Along with earning points, users accumulate badges based on their Foursquare activity. Badges can be awarded for the number of points you have accumulated, the frequency with which you check in to a category of place—such as university campus locations—or the number of other Foursquare users at a venue with you. Figure 7.3 shows an example of a badge.

Organizations are able to design and award their own badges for user activity, just as NASA did when astronaut Doug Wheelock checked in from space (Kincaid 2010). You can see the badges each user has earned when you view their profile, along with any tips they have left for other visitors of a particular venue, as shown in figure 7.4.

FIGURE 7.3
Campus Explorer badge on Foursquare

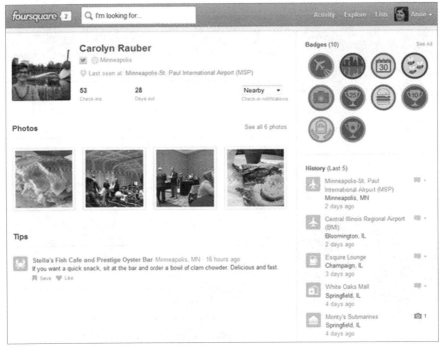

FIGURE 7.4
Foursquare profile with tips and earned badges

FIGURE 7.5
Photo integration

Foursquare encourages interaction by allowing both users and venue managers to upload photographs. When a user checks in at a location, they are automatically given the opportunity to upload a photo (fig. 7.5). Even after the user checks in, Foursquare gives them another opportunity to add a photo. Photos add visual impact to every part of the Foursquare experience and are strongly encouraged.

Populating Venues

Once you have established your account and explored Foursquare, it is time to create your venue. Before creating a location for your library in Foursquare, you should do a search for your library to see if a venue has already been created. Just because your library has not set up Foursquare does not mean that your library is not there or is not actively being used. Foursquare users can set up locations wherever they like, so be prepared to find venues representing different floors or rooms of your library. You can check by searching for your library name – or any nicknames your library may have—in either the search bar of the web interface or in the search icon of the mobile app or site.

If you do not find a location for your library, you have the option to add a new place to Foursquare, or you can use the "Add Venue" form at https://foursquare.com/add_venue. Foursquare provides guidelines for adding and editing venue information, which include naming and street address conventions (Foursquare 2010a). Venues with multiple locations or branches, such as public libraries, are discouraged from using suffixes in their location names. Instead of "Municipal Library—Main Branch," for example, Foursquare recommends simply writing "Municipal Library." Many public libraries use suffixes to identify the branch name; however, the location description and street address are more appropriate ways to identify the branch.

Academic libraries, on the other hand, often have recognizable names, such as Carnegie Library of the Syracuse University Libraries, shown in figure 7.6. In this instance, the name of the individual library should be used, rather than the name of the library system. Use common sense when choosing a naming

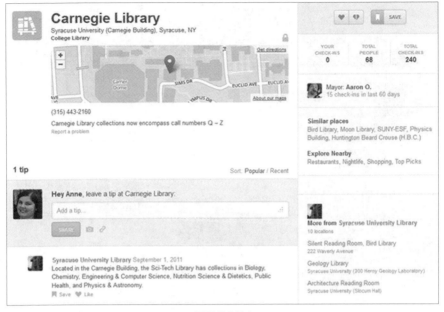

FIGURE 7.6
Foursquare venue page for Carnegie Library

convention—remember that you want your users to recognize the name of your library when they go to check in.

In addition to the style guide, Foursquare has House Rules, a set of community-developed guidelines and best practices. Most of these guidelines are for the end user who is checking in to a venue. However, one guideline deals with venue creation etiquette: do not create venues that do not exist (Foursquare 2011). Foursquare is intended to represent only physical locations, while tips can be used to represent the events and services taking place there. For example, you can create a venue for your exhibit space but don't create a venue for the specific exhibit in that space this month.

Once you add your library or determine that your library already exists on Foursquare, you now have to claim it as a venue. Claiming a venue makes you the Foursquare manager of that venue. Once you are the manager of your library venue, you can change listing information, such as the address and the hours that your library is open. Managers can also access analytics about who is checking in to your venue and when. To claim your library venue, search for your library's name and look at the venue page. On the bottom of the page there is a link that

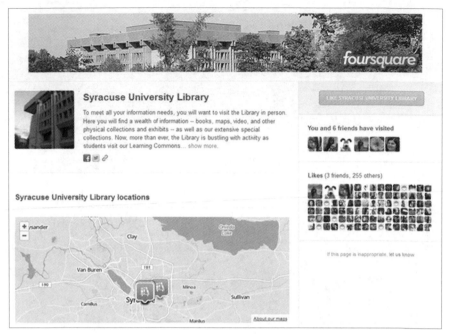

FIGURE 7.7
Foursquare brand page for Syracuse University Library

says, "Do you manage this location? Claim here." This link takes you to a form where you verify that you are an employee of the venue or are working on behalf of the venue. Once you fill out the form, there is a second verification step done by either mail or telephone.

Foursquare has different forms for claiming one location, ten or more locations, or one hundred or more locations. The forms are intended to help managers of multiple venues claim all their locations at once. These forms are particularly helpful if you have a number of library branches or multiple locations within your library that you would like to organize under one library system. When filling out a form to claim multiple venues, you will be asked to set up a brand page and enter the Foursquare URLs of the venues that you would like to add to that brand. Your brand page is an overarching page for your organization that points to all the venues in that organization. The Syracuse University Library (fig. 7.7) is an excellent example of a unified brand.

Once you are a verified manager of your library and its venues, it is time to start populating the venues with information. If you set up a brand page, the information you add to that page will also appear on each individual location. It is best to keep the brand information more general and make sure that it applies to your entire organization, not just to one location. Good things to add to your brand page include a link to your library's website, brief information about the library, and the services and resources for patrons.

You can use the individual venue pages to list library hours for each branch and the specific collections, services, or resources available there. At the Syracuse University Library, different libraries hold different call number ranges; the range information is included in each venue description. Syracuse University Library also uses the tips feature to notify patrons about events going on in the library and to respond to user comments. Carnegie Library notifies patrons that calculators are available with the Math Collection, while the Bird Library uses tips to respond to check-in comments complaining about noise by pointing patrons to quiet study spaces.

While setting up your venue pages, you may find duplicate venues. If Foursquare was actively used by your users before your library decided to manage the venues, there may be multiple user-created venues for your library. They may all have the same name or a nickname could be used. For example, "Club Bird" is a popular nickname given to Bird Library at Syracuse University. By merging the "Club Bird" venue into the "Bird Library" venue, users who search for "Club Bird" are automatically taken to the Bird Library page to check in there. While editing an individual venue, see the "Advanced Tools" section for instructions on how to merge duplicate venue pages.

After you establish your venue pages, consider adding some photos. Libraries can upload photos when leaving a tip or they can use a feature called "local updates." Updates are another way to push information to the users in a way that display more prominently than tips. An update appears when a user checks into or views the location which allows an image to be added. Since it is a low-cost means of promotion, any library can quickly add value to its Foursquare page with effective use of photos.

Another privilege that you have as a venue manager is to create "specials." A special is a reward that Foursquare users receive for checking in to your venue. Specials can be customized, such as one that can be unlocked by every person who checks in to your venue, or you can award specials to loyal visitors after a certain number of check-ins. Examples of specials include discounts for new customers or a loyalty gift, such as a free cup of coffee (Foursquare 2012b).

Libraries should think creatively about how to apply specials to their venues. In April 2011, University of Southern California Libraries gave a free book to users who checked in at select campus libraries (Masters 2011). USC Libraries also offered the libraries' mayors free membership to the Friends of the USC Libraries. The University of Kansas Libraries gave away flash drives to users who checked in to three campus libraries from August 19, 2011 to September 19, 2011 (University of Kansas Libraries 2011). The first example is what Foursquare refers to as a "Check-in Special": it is awarded to anyone who checks in. The second example is a "Mayor Special": it is awarded to the mayor. The third is a "Loyalty Special," as it encourages repeat check-ins (Foursquare 2013).

Navigating all the possibilities can be tricky but Foursquare has support available. If you have questions or run into problems, visit the Help Center (http://support.foursquare.com) or tweet your question to Foursquare support, @4sqSupport.

Maintaining and Advertising

After creating a Foursquare account and taking on the management duties of your venue, it is time to plan for the maintenance of your venue. By looking at other libraries' Foursquare pages, you will see that there are many different approaches to maintaining this social media tool. There are libraries that have not claimed their venues but have created a library account and comment on the activities taking place in their online space. Other libraries have claimed their venues and update the location information, although they do not interact with their Foursquare patrons. There are also libraries that frequently interact with patrons and carefully maintain their online locations. All are valid ways of using Foursquare. How you use this tool should be determined by the amount of time you are willing to invest in it and the frequency with which your library users engage with the tool.

There are a variety of suggestions for maintaining your venues. These recommendations should be considered when engaging library patrons with any social media tool, not just Foursquare. The first recommendation is to have a backup plan in case you can no longer manage your library's Foursquare account. If you use a library account, provide log-in information and training to another staff member. If you use a personal account, add a second administrator to your Foursquare venues. Even if that person is not interested in actively participating in managing your Foursquare engagement, it is a good idea to have someone who can back you up or who can reassign administrator rights to the tool if you change positions.

Once you have a back-up plan in place, decide on the types of interactions you want to have—or are willing to have—on Foursquare. Are you going to offer your own tips or are you going let library patrons leave all the tips for each other? Are you going to engage with patrons who use this space to complain about library services? Are you going to take those complaints as seriously as you would an e-mail? Are you going to report what the library has done to fix the complaints and issues of Foursquare, or you are going to publicize the resolutions through another venue?

Additional facets of your management plan should include the frequency and content of your venue's updates. Are you willing to update Foursquare, and any other social medial tools you are using, every time there is a change at your library? If you add a tip about an event at your venue, should you remove it once the event has taken place? If you are concerned about keeping your venue page current, do not include highly variable information unless you plan to update the page frequently. For example, Syracuse University does not include library hours, which shift at different points in the semester, on each library location in Foursquare. Instead, each venue contains a link to the library website where current hours are always listed on the home page.

Now that you have your venues set up and a plan to keep them up to date, it is time to promote your Foursquare presence. You can add a Foursquare badge to your website or include it on your contact page if you list other social media accounts there. You can also place a Foursquare window cling on your library entrance—Foursquare will send you a free window cling when you claim your venue that lets patrons know that you are participating in Foursquare when they enter your building. These are a sample of options that your management plan should address. Be prepared to revise the plan as other items arise or as assessment and evaluation dictate. You should also remain aware of trends in social media.

An additional way to promote your presence on Foursquare is to leave tips at other venues when there is a relevant connection between your two venues. For instance, if there is a theater production taking place in your community, you can leave a comment at that location pointing visitors to the library to find the book on which the play is based. Similarly, if you see students complaining about writing a research project in a campus study space, you can remind them to visit the library for research help. Next time a student checks in to that space, they will see your reminder to ask a librarian for help.

Evaluating, Assessing, and Using Statistics

Many of us are familiar with collecting a variety of data for libraries. Circulation numbers, e-resource usage statistics, and library webpage data inform libraries where best to dedicate resources and energy. Foursquare also provides data about your venue and automatically analyzes and displays it graphically. In the same way that circulation statistics communicate use patterns, Foursquare analytics, which are provided free of charge, will help your library identify behavior patterns in your Foursquare user population.

It will take some time to accumulate enough data to make full use of the Foursquare analytics features, but once your venue or brand has sufficient data, the analytics are quite robust. Remember that the data differ from more traditional webpage analytics in two important ways. First, Foursquare does not report interactions with the page, except to record data about check-ins. It does not track the number of photos uploaded over time, although it will tell you when a photo is uploaded, and it will not tell you how many times your venue page was viewed. Second, Foursquare stats are recorded at a much more granular level than traditional usage statistics. You can see a breakdown by gender and how many first time check-ins occurred over a week.

According to Foursquare support (Foursquare 2010b), you can expect to see data reporting:

1. Most recent visitors
2. Most frequent visitors
3. Time of day people check in
4. Total number of unique visitors
5. Graphics describing check-ins per day
6. Gender and age breakdowns for customers
7. The portion of Foursquare check-ins broadcast to Twitter and Facebook

Log in to your Foursquare account to access analytics for your venue or brand. Make sure that you are using Foursquare as the location or brand for which you want to see statistics. Hover the mouse over the name in the top right of the screen and select the account you wish to control. The toolbar at the top of the page contains a "Dashboard" button. Click this button to view and download statistics. If you manage only one venue, you will see only the statistics for that venue. If you manage multiple venues, you will see an option to view statistics for one or all venues you manage.

The dashboard provides two statistics categories: real-world analytics and long-term engagement. Click "View Report," to see detailed statistics in each of these categories, shown in figure 7.8. Real-world analytics statistics consist of:

- Total check-ins
- Number of check-ins shared over Twitter and Facebook
- Unique customers
- First time customers

- Top visitors
- Recent visitors
- Recent mayors
- Demographics

Long-term engagement statistics include:

- People who liked your venue
- People who liked your updates

- People who liked your tips
- People who saved your lists

Some statistics take time to accumulate; others require your involvement to create. In order to count people who have liked your updates, for example, you need to have posted some updates. Additionally, long-term engagement statistics will not appear until sufficient data has been collected. Weekly stats are also delivered to each manager's e-mail address, an example of which is shown in figure 7.9. These statistics include total number of check-ins for the week and breakdowns according to the day of the week, user gender, and the nature of check-in (first time versus

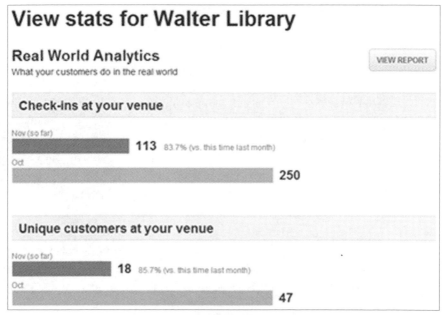

FIGURE 7.8
Foursquare report example

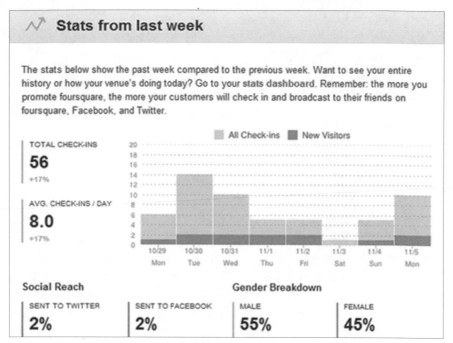

FIGURE 7.9
Weekly statistics e-mail from Foursquare

repeated). These weekly e-mails also identify "top customers" who have checked in most frequently over the last sixty days.

Foursquare statistics provide hard data about who uses Foursquare in the library, when, and how often. Assessing the impact of Foursquare with these data should be informed by your user population, how they interact with Foursquare, and the questions you are trying to answer. Foursquare's analytics can be used as its own assessment tool, and you can combine the statistics with statistics from other social media platforms. However, using Foursquare statistics on their own to draw far-reaching conclusions, unless the user base is very broad and engaged, is discouraged due to a high likelihood of sampling bias.

On the other hand, these statistics may give some insight into the specific population that uses Foursquare. Noticing patterns related to the number of check-ins per time of day or per day of the week may inform decisions about when to offer specials or post local updates. Following these statistics with other formal or informal assessments, measuring how many specials were redeemed, or determining how users heard about an event or gathering would provide additional insight into how Foursquare is used in your library.

FIGURE 7.10
Foursquare venue page for New York Public Library

SUCCESS STORY: NEW YORK PUBLIC LIBRARY

The New York Public Library (NYPL) main branch sits in Midtown Manhattan at the intersection of Fifth Avenue and 42nd Street. The building is a historical and cultural landmark that attracts many millions of people every year (New York Public Library 2010). A visitor might pose in a picture next to the famous marble lions guarding the entrance, visit the Main Reading Room and snap an artsy image of the book-lined walls, stop by the gift shop to purchase a finger puppet, or attend a reading by the author Don DeLillo in the Celeste Bartos Forum. Many visitors to the New York Public Library main branch have done all these things and have left a record of their activities on the NYPL's Foursquare venue page. As of this writing, over twenty-one thousand individuals have checked in at the main branch of the Library. The location itself has received more than thirty-four thousand check-ins, and users have uploaded nearly 1,500 photographs taken in or around the library. Figure 7.10 shows a screenshot of the NYPL's Foursquare page.

The New York Public Library is an example of a Foursquare success story. The library has engaged in Foursquare at all levels, including:

1. Creating a brand for the library system
2. Claiming and managing each branch library venue page
3. Uploading photographs and adding tips
4. Creating specials
5. Partnering with Foursquare to create a badge

While these features may not be viable or desirable for every academic, public, school, or special library interested in using Foursquare to market their services, we have seen that libraries have many of the same tools and opportunities available to them. With the Foursquare features previously discussed in mind, we can see how the NYPL puts it all together to create a very effective marketing tool.

The NYPL has a physical location in Manhattan, open to visitors and members of the public, and wants to market its space and services. However, the Manhattan branch is only one location in a larger library system; thus, the NYPL system has created a brand page, shown in figure 7.11, establishing itself as a one organization with many branches.

The branch libraries, including the NYPL main branch, are claimed as individual venues. Each branch could have claimed its library building venue and been added to the NYPL brand, or the NYPL brand could have claimed each venue. As we have seen, claiming a venue gives its manager control over some of the venue page content, access to the Foursquare analytics, and the ability to add updates and create specials (Foursquare 2012a). The New York Public Library is a contributor on its own venue page, uploading photographs, adding tips about the location, and posting local updates.

Users can like the NYPL's brand page, an equivalent to following on Twitter or liking on Facebook. When users like the page, the events and specials that the NYPL System promotes will appear on the user's activity feed. On the brand page, the NYPL's locations are visible, as are tips and photographs uploaded from all of its branches.

Similar information is available on the individual venue pages, including the position of the venue on a map, photos, and tips about the specific location. Visitors to the main branch of the NYPL have left many tips about the building's architecture, the availability of free Internet access, and even how to move chairs silently in the reading room. The NYPL has written a number of tips, including one tip advertising tours.

The NYPL main branch page highlights an active special that the library is promoting. The NYPL offers a special for every check-in: a 10 percent discount on

FIGURE 7.11
Foursquare brand page for New York Public Library

purchases in the gift shop. For libraries without a gift shop, a little creativity must be employed to make use of specials, and as long as staff members are aware of Foursquare specials, these can be applied to anything from coffee shop purchases to ticketed events, and even to Friends of the Library memberships.

In 2011, NYPL was the first library to offer a Foursquare badge, celebrating the library's one-hundredth anniversary (New York Public Library 2011). The "NYPL Centennial" badge is awarded to Foursquare users who check in at three NYPL branches or check in at the main branch five times. Foursquare is extremely selective in the badges they choose to support, and they do charge for the creation of a badge; however, if your library can pitch a compelling reason why Foursquare should partner with you, the badge option is available and can be an effective marketing tool.

The NYPL main branch is a strong example of a successful Foursquare page and libraries should adapt its success, and the successes of other libraries, to their own user population and library spaces. Foursquare encourages users to interact with the unique attributes of individual locations; the candid nature of users' tips and photos allow library staff to see the library through the eyes of their most loyal and engaged patrons.

BEST PRACTICES AND CONCLUSIONS

Throughout this chapter, we have made some suggestions for effective use of Foursquare in a library. We would like to reiterate some of those points here and to provide additional suggestions for making the most of this tool.

When setting up a Foursquare management plan at your library, be sure that more than one person can edit your Foursquare venues in case the primary manager is unavailable or changes jobs. While Foursquare provides many statistics on your venue's use, be sure to remember the limitations of these statistics and be wary of using them on their own for large-scale assessment and decision making. Using these statistics is a good way to understand how your Foursquare users interact with your virtual and physical venue; however, until you reach a critical mass of users, such as the NYPL, the user base may be too small to draw widespread conclusions. For best results, combine Foursquare statistics with other types of assessments in order to make decisions for your library. Additional assessment of your Foursquare users, such as surveys, may help further understand their motivations for using the tool and how Foursquare enhances their library experience.

One of the best features of Foursquare for libraries is the ways in which it incentivizes users to interact with your venue. Foursquare motivates users to accumulate points and earn badges by checking in; thus, they are gaining something from interacting with your library venue without necessarily requiring you to provide additional incentives.

Foursquare is a great marketing tool for library services and resources as well. In the Foursquare environment, an engaged business makes for a more engaged patron and it is easy for libraries to get in on the game and to stay connected with their users.

REFERENCES

Foursquare. 2010a. "What Is the Style Guide for Adding and Editing Venues?" November 15. http://support.foursquare.com/entries/214565-what-is-the-style-guide-for-adding-and-editing-venues.

Foursquare. 2010b. "What Are Analytics?" June 16. http://support.foursquare.com/entries/196050-what-are-analytics.

Foursquare. 2011. "House Rules." January 10. Last updated 2013. https://foursquare.com/info/houserules.

Foursquare. 2012a. "What Does It Mean to Claim My Location?" June 9. http://support.foursquare.com/entries/191108-what-does-it-mean-to-claim-my-venue.

Foursquare. 2012b. "Creating a Special." July 19. http://support.foursquare.com/entries/21751248-How-to-Create-a-Special.

Foursquare. 2013. "What Are Foursquare Specials?" February 25. http://support.foursquare.com/entries/481486-What-are-the-different-types-of-specials-.

Kincaid, J. 2010. "Houston, We've Had a Check-In: NASA Astronaut Just Used Foursquare from Space." October 22. http://techcrunch.com/2010/10/22/foursquare-space-astronaut/.

Leo, A. 2011. "Foursquare Badges: The Ultimate Guide." *Huffington Post*. April 19. www.huffingtonpost.com/2010/04/19/foursquare-badges_n_542985.html#s82329&title=Beginner_Badges.

Masters, N. 2011. "Unlock Foursquare Specials at the USC Libraries." April 7. http://dotsx.usc.edu/newsblog/index.php/main/comments/earn_badges_and_specials_by_checking_into_the_usc_libraries_on_foursqu/.

New York Public Library. 2010. "History of the New York Public Library." Last updated 2013. www.nypl.org/help/about-nypl/history.

New York Public Library. 2011. "The New York Public Library Partners with Foursquare to Unveil A New 'Badge.'" March 30. www.nypl.org/press/press-release/2011/03/30/new-york-public-library-partners-foursquare-unveil-new-%E2%80%9Cbadge%E2%80%9D.

University of Kansas Libraries. 2011. "KU Libraries Launch Foursquare Special." August 19. www.lib.ku.edu/news/2011/foursquare.html.

Using Blogs to Market Library Services and Resources

Carrie Moore, Julia Stringfellow, Amy Vecchione,
and Memo Cordova, Boise State University

A HISTORY AND CURRENT STATE OF BLOGS

Self-described as "the leading blog search engine and directory website," Technorati (n.d.) has kept track of blogs since 2004. The website publishes a yearly report on blogs, "Technorati's State of the Blogosphere," which consistently provides the most comprehensive and reliable metric for measuring the growth and evolution of blogs. The initial 2004 report stated that over "12,000 new weblogs [are] being created each day, which means that on average, a new weblog is created every 7.4 seconds" (Sifry 2004). These yearly reports attest that blogging has remained a constant and growing publishing tool. Nielsen reported, "By the end of 2011, NM Incite, a Nielsen/McKinsey company, tracked over 181 million blogs around the world, up from 36 million only five years earlier in 2006." (Nielsen 2012). Clearly blogs are not going away anytime soon. The term *weblog* was coined by Jorn Barger in 1997 "to describe the list of links on his Robot Wisdom website that 'logged' his internet wanderings" (Wortham 2007).

The meteoric rise of social media in the last few years provides an unprecedented array of tools that allows anyone with a computer to instantly self-publish content. Social media can be defined as "online technologies and practices that people use to share opinions, insights, experiences, and perspectives" (Rush 2012). Libraries leverage these tools to market to their users and keep them engaged with the library. While maintaining a comprehensive and unified list of current blogging libraries is challenging, Bar-Ilan (2012) found that "in December 2003, 157 active blogs were located and in February 2005 this number grew to 470; 299% growth in 14 months." In addition to these numbers, Bar-Ilan also mentioned that "at the end of December 2003, the Open Directory listed 5,373 blogs in different categories. From this list, 328 were classified as library and information science blogs (including personal blogs of librarians and information professionals); thus, library and information science blogs constituted 6% of the total number of blogs listed." In spite of the emergence of the new social media tools, such as Facebook, Twitter, and Pinterest, blogs remain a steady, if overshadowed, mainstay of communication. Singel (2010) reported that "blogging by teenagers has fallen by half since 2006, and even young adults seem to be dropping the habit." However, given the malleable definition of what blogging may mean to others, the "central vision of blogging—give citizens a nearly cost-free online printing press and let them make media—hasn't died" (Singel 2010). Young adults aside, the use of blogs has remained a reliable communication medium for individuals and corporations alike—from Fortune 500 companies to individuals who want to share their passion in their own voice.

116

This chapter provides an introduction to using blogs for marketing, discusses popular types of blog software, offers considerations for selecting software, and presents best practices for establishing and maintaining blogs. Examples of high-quality marketing blogs of libraries are presented as well.

USING BLOGS FOR MARKETING

Libraries strive to stay current with information trends in order to meet users' needs, which is why they investigate many new social media options to determine which ones are viable communication tools for the library. As stated earlier, blogging became a popular communication tool in the early 2000s, and libraries began investigating this tool as a way to meet patron expectations. Libraries that maintain blogs are nurturers by definition, and cheerleaders of library resources by choice. Many libraries embraced the blogging lifestyle soon after blogging became a steady and recognized form of marketing content. The Alberstons Library blog's first post was on January 17, 2006, where we stated, "Our aim is to showcase news and resources available in Albertsons Library to the Boise State University campus and the greater Treasure Valley community" (Cordova 2006). During this time, weblogs were just beginning to emerge as a "must have" online communication tool for college and public libraries. To our knowledge, the @thelibrary blog was the first academic library blog in Idaho.

Blogs meet the long-form information need in social media. Unlike Facebook and Twitter, which provide brief pieces of information, blogging allows for more content to be disseminated. Having a blog allows the library to disseminate information in a timely manner. In a matter of a few minutes, the latest and greatest library information can be typed into a post and shared with patrons. Updates regarding the building, upcoming events, completed programs, featured new resources, or just fun stuff to keep the patrons interested are some examples of content for blog posts. Blogs permit patrons to communicate and give feedback to the library via commenting on posts and sharing their experiences.

Setting the tone—formal or casual—for the library's blog is important, and may vary from contributor to contributor. Knowing the administration's or governing body's policy regarding how the library should be represented in an online environment is a critical component to consider when writing blog content. Research shows that patrons feel more connected to a personal tone of writing and stories that they can relate to (Steiner 2012). Posting pictures and varying the length of the posts is encouraged. Posts can be a few sentences of newsworthy content, such as "the parking lot is being repaved this Saturday," while other posts might be longer when trying convey instructions; for instance, how to use a library resource, such as the library catalog.

Patrons also like to see their names featured in the blog. Examples of patron naming include posting top readers during a summer reading program or volunteers working on a project. Readers also like to know about librarians and feel a personal connection with them. Librarians can post about their favorite types of reading materials, hobbies, or recent travels. By having staff from all departments of your library contribute blog posts, whether from reference, circulation, web team, archives, or administration, your blog will appeal to more readers and encourage interaction.

CHOOSING BLOG SOFTWARE

Choosing the best blog platform to use for any library may seem to be an overwhelming task. There is a plethora of platforms available, and they are constantly being created, being updated, or going away. It is important to evaluate the different platforms available based on the needs of the library. The platform chosen ultimately depends on your purpose, intended audience, features needed, ease of adding posts, and comment availability, as well as other considerations.

Using a search engine and search terms such as *"blog platforms"*, *"blog platform reviews"*, and *"library blogs"* brings up a wealth of different blog platforms that can be compared side by side. Blog users are not shy about sharing their opinions of different platforms. Contacting peer libraries to find out which platforms they use, how they chose it, and how effective it has been helps greatly in choosing the platform. Posting a question on regional, state, or national library organizations' listservs can lead to useful information. Choosing one of the more popular platforms that patrons and library staff may already be familiar with is also beneficial.

Consider the features below when evaluating the different blog platforms:

- Cost (if any) to use the platform
- Ease of setup
- Ease of navigation
- Ease of linking to the library's website
- Ability to regulate timing of new blog postings
- Ability to archive old posts
- Ability to search within the blog
- Access for readers to add comments to the posts
- Functionality to add categories and search terms to the posts
- Prominent display of posting dates
- Recent entries showing at the top of the blog
- Ability to add links and posts to other social networking sites

Selecting a Platform

While there are many blogging platforms out there to choose from as shown above, it is important to select the platform that best meets your library's needs and audiences. The best platform option varies from library to library when taking into account your user needs, the purpose of your blog, the expected size of your blog, and other factors. Be sure to examine especially the needs of the prospective users and the purpose of the blog when selecting a platform.

Popular Blogging Platforms

Five of the current blogging platforms most commonly used by libraries are described below, with some discussion on the strengths and weaknesses of each. The platform plays a major role in the blog's theme and tone. The ability to access and edit a blog through a mobile device is also an important factor to consider when researching blog platforms. Performing a Google search of the platforms described below will bring up numerous reviews of the platform, its features, and its accessibility through mobile devices.

Blogger

Blogger (www.blogger.com) is a blogging service owned by Google that, naturally, integrates easily with Google Analytics. Users can create a free blog through the user-friendly setup wizard and also have the ability to select their own domain name. The Blogger platform is used by businesses and professional associations, although the majority of its users have personal blogs. Anyone with a Gmail account can create a blog; there is no limit to the number of blogs you can create using your Google ID. Other Blogger blogs can be followed, and the blogger's dashboard provides alerts when any other blogs have new posts. The dashboard also displays statistics for the blog. Blogger is also one of the more strict platforms when it comes to spamming. An example of a library that uses this type of platform is the Ashland University Library blog (fig. 8.1). Posts are frequently added to this blog—sometimes several posts a week—and topics include updates on how the

ASHLAND LIBRARY NEWS

A site for news about the Library at ASHLAND UNIVERSITY in Ohio and a resource for current students

THURSDAY, NOVEMBER 15, 2012

Update: Library Systems Upgrade

At 11 am today (11/15) AU Library systems will be down for a scheduled upgrade.

We anticipate this outage lasting through the afternoon. During this time there will be no online circulation functions, patron authentication or OhioLINK borrowing available.

- Off line circulation will be in place; pick-up and check out books as usual.
- Please use the OhioLINK catalog to locate books and other resources.
- Library account information will be processed after the upgrade is complete.
- Contact the AU Library circulation desk if you have questions at x5400.

Updates will be posted here, on the AU Library Facebook page and via the IRC Twitter feed. Thank you in advance for your patience during this time.

ASHLAND UNIVERSITY LIBRARY

LIBRARY HOURS: FALL 2012

AU Library's Fall hours schedule begins Monday, August 20th. Exceptions to regular operating hours are detailed on the Library Hours & Updates page.

- Monday - Thursday
  7:45 am to 11:00 pm

FIGURE 8.1
Ashland Library News, the blog for Ashland University Library

library is using different types of social media, library events and hours updates, and book awards. Concise posts and the right amount of images give this particular blog a clean, easy-to-follow look.

Blogger also provides the ability to edit the blog using a mobile device. It has apps for mobile devices available through Google Mobile (www.google.com/mobile/blogger). The features of the apps include the ability to add posts, attach photos, enter location information, and view a listing of all your posts. The app is easy to use and includes a plain-text editor.

Of the platforms mentioned above, the easiest to maintain is the Blogger platform especially for those libraries that use Google apps and Gmail for e-mail accounts. Blogger has worked very well for Albertsons Library at Boise State University for these very reasons.

WordPress

WordPress (http://wordpress.org) is a nonhosted platform and, depending on the person asked, the most popular content management system currently available. It is an open-source system with numerous free templates and themes. WordPress includes an extensive plug-in library that allows users to expand the blog beyond the basic architecture. It also provides tutorials and forums that are easy to follow while creating the blog. WordPress is widely utilized for personal and business use to create both blogs and websites integrated with blogs. Blogs created through WordPress generally have a more professional look and greater functionality. The Sheridan Libraries use WordPress for their blog (blogs.library.jhu.edu/wordpress).

WordPress also has free apps for mobile devices (wordpress.org/extend/mobile). The apps are smaller simulations of the WordPress platform and make accessing and editing the blog from a mobile device easy to do. Most of the platform's features can be accessed through the app, including the ability to view and write posts, upload photos and videos, manage comments, and look up the blog's stats. Based on user reviews, the apps for WordPress are some of the easiest ones to use for blogging.

Drupal

Drupal (http://drupal.com) is a content management system that is also free to set up. This system is used for blogs of both personal and business use. Drupal's extensions, called contrib modules, allow users to add different features to their blog and increase functionality. Some knowledge of PHP (a popular scripting language) may be needed in order to use the system's advanced features. The Harris County

Public Library blog uses Drupal as its platform (www.hcpl.net/blog). Posts are not published in chronological order, which makes the blog challenging to follow, but the posts and use of images are well done.

Compared to other blog platforms, the mobile apps for Drupal are not as user friendly, and editing a blog from a mobile device can be challenging. User reviews of the mobile options for Drupal aren't too promising; they include reports that the apps often crash when trying to access content or add a new blog post. Simple text posting is the main feature of Drupal apps.

Typepad

Typepad (www.typepad.com) is a hosted site used for both personal and professional purposes. This software requires a paid subscription, which provides customers with access to a domain name, customized blog designs, and personal support, as well as a comprehensive help section. Typepad blogs generally have a classic, professional look.

Typepad also features a Micro version, which is a microblogging platform that easily integrates with Facebook. The Kansas State University Libraries use Typepad for their blog (ksulib.typepad.com/talking). Their blog includes information on library and university events, resources, instructional videos, and information for writing papers and citing sources. A series of posts called "Short Cuts" provides useful and concise information on university and library resources.

The mobile app for Typepad is free. Its features are not as versatile as those of Blogger or WordPress, but they do include the ability to add posts and photos, and to add a post in draft mode before making it public.

Of the platforms mentioned above, the easiest to maintain is the Blogger platform, especially for those libraries that use Google apps and Gmail for e-mail accounts. Blogger has worked very well for Albertsons Library at Boise State University for these very reasons.

ESTABLISHING AND MAINTAINING A BLOG

A well-received and effective blog requires a few more steps in order to become fully realized. Maintenance of the blog is also vital. The steps below will help guide you through these processes.

Set a Social Media Strategy

One of the main factors to consider before establishing the blog is deciding how to connect the blog posts to the library's existing social media strategy. If an overarching strategy is not already in place, you can create and develop one at the same time that you initiate your blog. The first aspect of a social media strategy involving a blog is to determine who the primary bloggers will be. The maintenance of the blog and assigning the person or team who will be responsible for the posts is one of the most important discussions in developing a social media strategy. The primary bloggers will be those individuals responsible for adding posts when there is substantial news about the library and who respond to comments posted by patrons. Additionally, they will be the ones who delegate the need for a response to an appropriate person if a referral is required. Adding everyone to the blog who is interested in contributing is important in order to ensure adequate types of and sufficient content for the interest of the users; however, the bloggers must be trained on the strategies, style, and content of the blog. As a result, another role of the primary bloggers is to share this information with the other bloggers and review drafts before they are posted. The roles of primary bloggers may change as your library evolves and responsibilities shift.

As noted earlier, blogging is currently the most popular social media technology that allows long-form messages and information to be distributed to patrons. Albertsons Library at Boise State University is one example of an academic library creating a social media strategy and a blog. Over time Boise State has utilized two different social media strategy guidelines when developing blog content. The social media strategy at Albertsons Library was at first quite casual. The team appointed two librarians to take the lead in using social media tools to promote the library, including Facebook, Twitter, and blogging. The blog had one primary blogger whose role was to add content when no other posts were scheduled, as well as to review all posts for consistency, style, and scope. A tertiary responsibility was following up with user comments and promoting the blog.

The simple strategy was successful for some time; however, it became apparent that it was necessary to revisit the strategy due to a lack of fresh content. Other librarians wanted to contribute but were unsure how to post and about the types of content to share. As a result, a more defined social media strategy was created. The new strategy included specific types of content with timelines and an increased focus. The library team working with social media assembled and drafted guidelines for a strategy that met the needs of all the library units and involved all interested librarians.

Know Your Audience

Successful bloggers and other social mediasts know and understand the needs of their potential audience. Most blog software provides demographic information about types of browsers individuals are using and some geographic data, but cannot provide information about the individuals using the blog. It is helpful to gain information about the blog's audience by asking about the identity of the readers. Learning about the audience can be done in a number of ways: have blog readers complete a survey or enter a contest, or post questions on the blog that are easy for your patrons to answer in the comments section. Asking questions that are interesting to readers involves some trial and error, but will help with understanding your readers and the issues that they care about.

Choose Content

Determining the content of your blog is something that should be decided during social media strategy team meetings. The group should develop guidelines on what is appropriate content to post. Posting items that present the library in a positive light and encourage users to utilize the services and resources is beneficial. Remember, social media is marketing as much as it is engagement. Keep the posts informative as well as timely, and incorporate them into the social media strategy timeline to ensure users receive important and interesting content in a coordinated manner from all your social media outlets. Figure 8.2 provides an example from the Albertsons Library blog.

While occasional cross-posting among social media tools can be beneficial—for example, for holiday closures, new services, or anything that needs to be disseminated widely—it should be done judiciously to inform the audience and with a goal of bringing increased traffic to the blog. Having the blog automatically update Facebook, Twitter, or other social media accounts the library offers is discouraged because too much cross-posting can be redundant and thus frustrating to users, as they are looking for new and useful information (Solomon 2012). Use phrases that are appropriate to the platform when writing posts that link to the blog. Try to incorporate different words and phrasing that are engaging and enticing in order to meet the different needs of the users of your social media platforms.

If your library participates in national surveys, such as LibQual, or utilizes other assessment tools, use the comments section of the surveys as content for blog posts. This allows the library to respond to direct queries in order to educate the audience. Another way to find content is to look for the keywords that searchers

123

FIGURE 8.2
Blog post for Albertsons Library, Boise State University

use to find the blog, then fill in gaps between the website and user knowledge. Patrons may have landed on the blog trying to find information about a topic, but the blog may not address that topic directly. Providing posts on these topics will ameliorate information gaps.

Providing and sharing basic library information is crucial for any successful social media strategy. Although some information may seem like old news to librarians, often our users are unaware of vital content; one prime example of this is how to search a particular database. Posting general library information on a regular basis also helps the staff maintain the library's blog since there will always be content to add (Solomon 2011).

Populate Your Blog

A successful blog is nurtured with a steady flow of posts. However, there should be a balance in how many posts are offered in a day or week. Too many posts and the blog may contribute to the onslaught of information already there—your readers may tire of attempting to keep up, and thus vital information may be missed. Too few posts and there is a risk of losing the interest of the readers. There is no hard-and-fast rule about the frequency of blog posts, but once or twice a week is generally recommended. A good strategy is to have the posts ready to submit by writing a blog post one day of the week and keeping them ready to post the following week. It can also be helpful to write quick posts-to-be that can be expanded or timed accordingly. The Blogger software, along with some others, allows posts in draft form, and has the ability to post on a specific date and time. Avoid posting multiple times a day, unless the blog is covering conferences, events, or instances where more than one post is necessary to fully describe the event.

Maintain Your Blog

Blogs may be a mainstay of libraries, but it does not mean that the platforms or third-party applications that make blogging possible stay fixed or unchanged. Trends in social media take place rapidly; thus, the blogging platform used today may radically change the way posts are created. For instance, third-party applications may be abandoned or updated, or a specialized code may become no longer viable. These types of changes make it imperative that bloggers maintain an awareness of trends, best practices, and updates in the technology for their blog software. If using a specific platform, such as Blogger, keep abreast of changes via its own blog. Many times the platforms provide an advance preview or notices of changes in their templates, which third-party applications are no longer being supported, trends in blogging practices, and more. Staying aware of blogging technology in general is also very helpful in order to be aware of big-picture changes or innovations.

Contributors

An important aspect of maintaining a steady flow of content is to have librarians and interested staff members contribute posts. Libraries of all sizes have plenty of information resources, staff experiences, and day-to-day operations data to allow for a steady flow of blog-worthy material. It is recommended that a schedule with committed bloggers be established to ensure that posts are being continually produced and that contributors are committed to posting regularly. This schedule should be included in the social media strategy, and one person should be appointed to ensure that the schedule is followed.

ADVERTISING AND MARKETING A BLOG

A library blog may not necessarily be the first place interested patrons look online for information. How can you capture your users' attention? Key points to make the blog visible include the following:

- Link the blog's really simple syndication (RSS) feed to the library's homepage. Most blogging platforms provide a RSS feed of the blog's content. Services such as Twitterfeed (http://twitterfeed.com) can push the blog's RSS feed to websites or social media networks and make it available to news readers everywhere.
- Cross-post blog entries to social networks. If your library has a presence on social networks such as Facebook, Twitter, or Tumblr, link your posts as relevant. Be wary of duplicating too much of your content. Usually just having the link fed via RSS to various social networks is sufficient, unless there is an urgent message that needs to be shared.
- Allow comments. Comments are highly useful, as they allow readers to interact with the posts. The volume of comments will vary depending on the size and engagement level of the institution. It is best to monitor comments before allowing them to show up on the blog and it is also necessary to be aware of any legal implications of removing or not posting entries. Check with your legal department on this issue. Assign one or two people to monitor the comments, to respond to comments, and to maintain the flow of information to keep your readers engaged with the posts and commenting on them.
- Install third-party or native sharing icons on the blog. Blogger and WordPress already have "Share This" buttons that make sharing posts easy with other users and social networks.

EVALUATING AND ASSESSING BLOGS

Determining how to measure success is a critical piece of a library's social media strategy. Identifying benchmarks that define a social media tool's success is crucial in advocating for its continued use, including blogs. A benchmark example is establishing a set number of "times viewed" or of posted comments that the library considers successful.

When the Albertsons Library blog was first initiated, there were many pay-for-use tools to measure blog traffic but very few free services. Google Analytics and other third party applications provided rudimentary blog counters. Some of the earliest traffic metrics, which involved embedding bits of script to the blog's HTML code, provided the first statistics for January 2006: 691 page loads, 479 unique visitors, 332 first time visitors, and 147 returning visitors.

One free service that provides blog metrics is StatCounter. StatCounter became the primary blog metrics tools for the first few years of our blog. It was consistent and free, and could maintain traffic data for multiple blogs. Until Google Analytics emerged as a complete online service, StatCounter was our primary tool for blog traffic. Figure 8.3 provides an example of the @thelibrary's StatCounter dashboard from 2009 to 2012.

StatCounter provided a way to measure site visitors and page loads, but at the time, these more extensive features were provided only for a fee. After Google Analytics improved from the original beta version, it became the primary tool for measuring blog traffic and statistics at the Albertsons Library. However, StatCounter was retained in order to maintain a checks-and-balances feature when reporting traffic data for statistical purposes.

Google Analytics is a free service from Google and offers a comprehensive system to measure and analyze a wide range of metrics, such as user behaviors, demographics, browser and operating system used, devices, and much more (Claiborne 2011). It is important for libraries to consider using a metric system that illustrates a blog's reach with its users, as well as one that provides information about the users and their usage patterns. Google Analytics now has a variety of useful tools that measure emerging trends, such as the use of mobile devices regarding blog traffic, as noted in figure 8.4. Google Analytics offers rich and robust metrics tools to keep track of your visitors. It is a free product and highly recommended for all libraries.

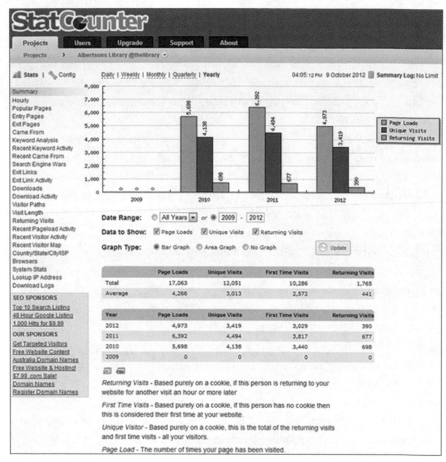

FIGURE 8.3
Statistics via StatCounter for the Albertsons Library blog,
Boise State University

Libraries can generate audience and patron comments by asking stimulating questions and promoting materials, resources, and services. Commenting on other blogs with related posts can also draw reader interest. Regularly reviewing and revising your social media strategy is necessary to keep it in alignment with the goals set by your library, any changes in audience, and updated technology. It is also important to have one person, or a very small group, assigned to ensure that the strategy and guidelines are being followed.

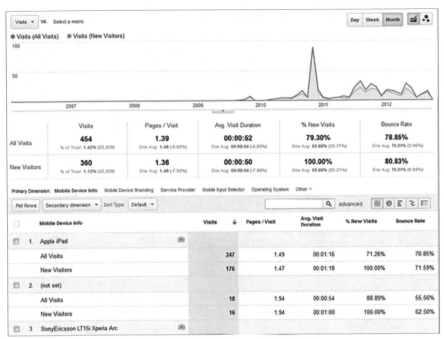

FIGURE 8.4
Google Analytics device information for the Albertsons Library blog,
Boise State University

BEST PRACTICES AND CONCLUSIONS

A library blog is a timely and useful venue to showcase library resources and services and is an important facet of a library's personality, particularly if that personality shines through the voice of its contributors. In evaluating the various blogging platforms and determining the best one to use for your library, it is important to take into account a variety of factors, such as the intended audience, user interface, ease of setup and cost, and how much staff time can be devoted to updating and maintaining the blog. Choosing the right blogging platform may seem daunting, but it is possible to choose by considering what your library hopes to achieve through implementing a blog and finding one that best meets those needs. As part of a social media strategy, the blog team also needs to determine how the blog will be used effectively to let your audience know about current resources and events happening at your library.

Blog post writers should use their own voice when discussing a particular library resource or service, as readers appreciate the tone and prose of an individual's informative post. Avoid the dry "public service announcement" that often plagues faceless entities. Keep the content "fresh" by posting on a regular schedule, and use multiple sources of information to generate ideas for blog post content. The development of a social media strategy for the library will help you establish and maintain your blog. The strategy needs to include evaluation and measures of success. Regular review and revision of this strategy is vital to keep up with changing technologies, user needs, and library goals.

REFERENCES

Bar-Ilan, Judit. 2012. "The Use of Weblogs (Blogs) by Librarians and Libraries to Disseminate Information." Information Research 12 (4). http://informationr.net/ir/12-4/paper323.html.

Claiborne, Trevor. 2011. "New Google Analytics: Improvements in Mobile Reporting." *Google Blog*. June 23. http://analytics.blogspot.com/2011/06/new-google-analytics-improvements-in_23.html.

Cordova, Memo. 2006. "Albertsons Library's Weblog: @thelibrary.".*@thelibrary* (blog). January 27. http://albertsonslibrary.blogspot.com/2006/01/albertsons-librarys-weblog-thelibrary.html.

Nielsen. 2012. "Buzz in the Blogosphere: Millions More Bloggers and Blog Readers." *Newswire* (blog). March 8. www.nielsen.com/us/en/newswire/2012/buzz-in-the-blogosphere-millions-more-bloggers-and-blog-readers.html.

Rush, Sharron. 2012. "Social Media." *W3C eGovernment Wiki*. www.w3.org/egov/wiki/Glossary#S.

Singel, Ryan. 2010. "Blogging 'Peaks,' but Reports of Its Death Are Exaggerated." *Wired*. December 16. www.wired.com/business/2010/12/long-live-blogging/.

Sifry, David. 2004. "State of the Blogosphere, October 2004." *Sifry's Alerts* (blog). October 10. www.sifry.com/alerts/archives/000245.html.

Solomon, Laura. 2012. "5 Reasons Why Your Library Shouldn't Be Cross-posting." *MeanLaura* (blog). June 28. www.meanlaura.com/archives/1508.

Solomon, L. 2011. *Doing Social Media So It Matters: A Librarian's Guide*. Chicago: American Library Association.

Steiner, Sarah K. 2012. *Strategic Planning for Social Media in Libraries*. Chicago: ALA TechSource.

Technorati. n.d. "About Technorati." http://technorati.com/about-technorati/.

Wortham, Jenna. 2007. "After 10 Years of Blogs, the Future's Brighter Than Ever." *Wired*. December 17. www.wired.com/entertainment/theweb/news/2007/12/blog_anniversary.

QR Codes and Libraries

Janet Hack, Hoover Library, McDaniel College

Ilana Kingsley, University of Alaska Fairbanks

Introduced in 1994 by the Japanese company Denso Wave Incorporated (Rouillard 2008), quick-response codes, commonly known as QR codes, have been incorporated into public, academic, special, and school library settings. Libraries are using QR codes in a variety of ways, including promotion of library resources, events and special collections; providing mobile access to instructional material; scavenger hunts and tours for library orientation; and access to electronic library resources from both in and outside the physical library; and more.

QR codes are similar to barcodes, but they are two dimensional and can hold ten to a hundred times more information than traditional bar codes (Denso 2001). Basically, QR codes are made up of black-and-white squares containing geometric shapes (Ashford 2010); however, some are in color and may have images embedded in the code. Mobile devices, such as tablets and smartphones, scan QR codes using the device's camera and a QR code reader application.

QR codes are considered a location-based technology because they link physical objects to digital information (Murphy 2012) and may be classified into the categories of information transfer and linking to the web (Whitchurch 2012). Information transfer does not require Internet access. Upon scanning a QR code, text-based information—such as phone numbers, event information, and contact information—is acquired from the QR code and displayed on the device. If the patron is within a cell phone or wireless signal, she may interact with the information received. For example, she may dial a phone number that the QR code displayed or send a text message to the number displayed. Linking to the web requires Internet access. After scanning a QR code, an Internet connection is made. The information displayed to the user may include websites, videos, podcasts, or any other content available via the web.

QR codes have become popular marketing tools in libraries, as well as in other educational and noneducational settings, because they are a no-cost to low-cost technology. Using free or fee-based generators available online, QR codes are easy to create, publish, and collect usage data.

This chapter focuses on how to successfully implement a QR code campaign in your library. Topics include information on how to create, maintain, and track QR codes; where to place them; how patrons locate and use QR codes; best practices; and case studies.

CREATING THE CODE

There are numerous online QR code generators. Choosing the right one depends on many factors, including the type of code you want (information transfer or web linking), whether you want to track code usage, and how much you are willing to pay for creating QR codes. Most of the QR code generators that allow tracking code usage are not free, nor do they allow easy tracking of informational QR codes. In order to track usage, these services most often generate a shortened URL that links to a webpage or other data source. This works well for QR codes linking to web pages, but it tends to defeat the purpose of informational QR codes. While it is possible to create informational QR codes with some of these systems, in actuality the QR code links to a short URL that then opens a text file, vCard, or other online data source, which means that even informational QR codes require an Internet connection.

There are a few points to remember when creating your codes. The more data encoded, the denser the code will be. This is one reason many QR code generators start out by creating a shortened URL. Higher density also means a larger QR code. Figure 9.1 shows two QR codes linking to LITA publications, both created with the same QR code generator. The code on the left uses the full URL, whereas the code on the right uses a shortened URL.

Some code generators let you choose the size of the code when you create it. Although QR codes can be resized—to a point—in order to fit your space requirements, try to select the size that best matches your needs when you create the code. The density of the code has a noticeable impact on the ability to resize the code;

FIGURE 9.1
QR codes: full URL versus shortened URL

FIGURE 9.2
Sizes of QR codes

FIGURE 9.3
Stretched QR codes

denser codes cannot be resized as much as less-dense codes can. When resizing a code, remember that it must remain square, and it must be displayed with a white border. It is best to test your code, preferably with several different devices, in order to make sure that it still works after resizing. Figure 9.2 demonstrates some of the different sizes for QR codes. The image on the left is a full-sized QR code. The other images have been resized. The second image should work on most devices, the third image may work on some devices, and the final image is too small to scan properly. Figure 9.3 shows the effect of stretching the QR codes. The code on the left may work on some devices, but the image on the right is too distorted to scan effectively.

Bitly

One popular free resource for creating trackable QR codes is bitly (https://bitly .com/). Registration is free, and while you are not required to create shortened URLs and QR codes, you must register if you want to track usage. Another advantage of registering with bitly is the ability to create groups of resources. Once you have created the shortened URL, or bitmark, you can download a QR code linking to the shortened URL. One drawback of this system is that patrons will see the shortened URL instead of the destination URL when they scan the QR code. bitly also does not allow for the creation of informational QR codes.

Creating QR Codes Using bitly

1. Log in to your account at https://bitly.com. If you do not have an account, you can create one. (You can generate QR codes without an account; however, if you want to track usage you will need to create an account and log in when generating codes.)
2. Enter a URL where it says "Paste a link here" to generate a bitmark (shortened URL).
3. To find the QR code, click on "Stats" in the top menu bar, then select your desired URL.
4. Click on the desired bitmark.
5. To the left of the shortened URL will be a small QR code. Click on this to view the code.
6. Right-click the image to copy or save the QR code.

myQR.co

Another free resource for creating trackable QR codes is myQR.co (http://myqr.co/). Registration is free and is not required for creating shortened URLs and QR codes, but if you want to track usage you must register. In addition to creating QR codes for web links, myQR.co also allows you to create messages, vCards, and maps. As noted earlier, while some of these appear to be informational QR codes, they are actually links to data files and do require an Internet connection. Unlike many other free QR code generators, myQR.co allows you to make colorful QR codes. If you elect to make colorful QR codes, remember that the barcode scanner is looking at the contrast between the light and dark pixels. The codes generally scan better with a light colored background and a darker, contrasting color in the foreground.

Creating QR codes with myQR.co

1. Create an account and log in to http://myqr.co/. As with bitly, you can generate QR codes without having an account, but if you want to track usage, you will need to create an account and log in before creating QR codes.
2. Select the type of QR code you want to create: website, message, contact, or map. Note that all QR codes generated through myQR.co require an Internet connection.
3. Enter the data you want to link to.
4. *Optional:* select background and foreground colors for your code.
5. Generate the code.
6. Download and save your code.

135

ZXing QR Code Generator

The ZXing (zebra crossing) QR code generator (http://zxing.appspot.com/generator) allows you to create several different code types, including contact information, text, calendar event, and URL. ZXing does not create shortened URLs, so longer web addresses can create fairly dense QR codes. Also, ZXing does not provide any mechanism for tracking usage. If you are looking to generate true informational QR codes that do not require an Internet connection, the ZXing generator is a good choice. ZXing also lets you create three different sizes of QR codes, with several levels of error correction.

Creating QR codes with ZXing

1. Go to http://zxing.appspot.com/generator.
2. Select the type of code you want to generate. Note that text QR codes are truly informational and do not require an Internet connection. Larger blocks of text generate denser QR codes and work best with larger codes.
3. Enter the data you want to display with your QR code.
4. Select the size code you want to generate.

5. Generate the code.
6. Download and save your code.

PLACING QR CODES FOR MARKETING

Effective placement of QR codes is limitless and should take place both inside and outside of your library. Placing QR codes in the library is a good start for marketing services and resources, as well as for offering self-paced tours. Several ideas for where QR codes may be placed within the physical library are listed below:

In the stacks. Add QR codes that link to specific books or a subject range of books onto posterboard or blocks. Place the posterboard or blocks in the stacks. This method of QR code placement is good for patrons who are browsing the stacks and may not be aware of books and resources available electronically.

On the ends of aisles. Place QR codes that link to subject guides, subject librarian contact information, the reference desk, chat, or SMS on the ends of aisles. Patrons seeking assistance in a specific subject area can use the QR codes to find more information about the subject or contact a librarian for additional help.

On or near equipment. Place QR codes that link to instructional videos or help guides about how to use equipment on or near the piece of equipment. This method of QR code placement is good for patrons who need help scanning, copying, printing, using microfiche, and so on.

On doors. Place QR codes containing contact information on doors throughout the library. Information stored on QR codes can include phone numbers and contact information for subject librarians or for room reservations.

The ideas listed above are only some examples of the many possibilities of where to place QR codes in the library. Another area of QR code placement to consider is outside of your library. Public libraries have been successful with placing QR codes that link to electronic books in airports, public transportation locations, and other offsite locations. Placement of QR codes outside of your library is a great tool for marketing services to patrons who do not physically access your library or who may not know what your library has to offer.

LOCATING AND USING QR CODES

In the physical world, patrons can look for QR codes on brochures, posters, table tents, window decals, or signs, and near machines, display cases, doors, and artwork. In the digital world, look for them embedded in web pages, social media pages, and online library catalogs.

Before you can scan a QR code, your mobile device needs to have a QR code reader installed; your device may already have one. If not, you can download a QR code reader from your mobile phone's application store. You can also visit mobile websites that choose the best reader for your phone, such as Link.Me (http://m .qmcodes.com/reader). To scan a QR code, hold your mobile device in front of or over the code. You may need to start the QR application before attempting to scan. Your mobile device will recognize the symbol and either display information or direct you to the appropriate link (Winter 2011).

Patrons should be conscious of what they scan because malicious QR codes may be affixed over legitimate ones (Waters 2012). Waters suggests that users of QR codes, especially those who own Androids, should scan QR codes only from sources that they are familiar with or that are from trustworthy entities. To help patrons determine legitimacy of a QR code, libraries should provide additional information about what to expect after scanning the code. For example, instead of just showing a QR code, include a sentence or two of what to expect, such as "This code will direct you to an instructional video on how to use the copy machine."

MAINTAINING AND ADVERTISING A QR CODE MARKETING CAMPAIGN

Once you have started using your QR codes, make sure that patrons know what they are and how to use them. Although QR codes are becoming more commonplace, they are still new enough that many people may not know what they are. For your initial campaign, you may want to include some text to encourage patrons to scan the codes. A simple "For more information, scan this with your smartphone" may be sufficient. It may also help to include an announcement in your library's blog, newsletter, Facebook page, or anywhere else you regularly post news. Murphy (2012) recommends an eye-catching display of QR codes in highly visible parts of the library in order to drive interest, while at the same time using smaller codes in more relevant areas or where you would normally post informational flyers.

QR codes require very little maintenance provided the encoded information does not change. If the URL or other information needs to be updated, you will most likely need to create a new code containing the new information. Some fee-based QR code generators, such as BeeTagg (www.beetagg.com) or Kaywa (http://qrcode.kaywa.com/), provide dynamic QR codes that allow you to update information without having to change the code. If you anticipate needing to frequently update information embedded in your codes, especially if you make heavy use of print materials, you may want to consider one of the aforementioned options.

If you do need to replace a QR code, remember to replace it everywhere it has been used. It is worth putting thought into the best content for and use of QR codes. Codes on webpages can be easily replaced by using the same file name for the new code and replacing the old file on your web server. You will also need to update the images you have embedded in Facebook, Google Places, and other online locations. If you use QR codes on print materials, reprint them with the new code.

If you post printed QR codes outdoors, bear in mind that many inks will run or smear in damp conditions, which could make your codes unscannable. Try to place your printed signs in sheltered areas or protect the codes so that they are weatherproof. Permanent or semipermanent signs should be professionally produced using weatherproof and fade-resistant materials (Whitchurch 2012). For temporary signs, you can protect the QR codes by laminating the signs or by covering the code with a piece of clear tape. As always, make a sample sign first and test the code to make sure it scans through the protective coating.

EVALUATING, ASSESSING, AND USAGE STATISTICS

As with any marketing campaign, assess the effectiveness of your QR codes. Standard evaluation techniques—surveys, direct observation, or even anecdotal evidence—can be used to evaluate usage of your QR codes. Informational QR codes, which do not require an Internet connection, are nearly impossible to track by other methods.

Web links and informational QR codes generated through a URL shortener are relatively easy to track and analyze. bitly and MyQR.co both provide the number of scans for your QR code. bitly breaks down usage by referrer (in case you are using the shortened URL in other web links), while MyQR.co does not; however, MyQR .co provides more detailed information about the devices used to scan your codes, so you can see, for example, how many patrons are using iOS and how many are using Android. Most paid QR code generators also provide analytics.

Web analytic tools, such as Google Analytics, can also be used to track QR code usage. These tools usually do not distinguish between scans and clicks; thus, if you are using the same URL for both a QR code and other web links, you will not be able to tell how many visits came from your QR code. One way to get around this situation is to use a different landing page for your QR code (Sekyere 2012).

One deficiency of both QR code generators and analytics tools is that they do not tell you where your patrons found your code. While some of the services give locational information, it is usually limited to country or IP address location. This is usually not going to tell you if a patron scanned a QR code on a poster outside your library, if they found a code embedded in your Facebook page, or if they used a code on a sign in the library stacks.

BEST PRACTICES

Before forging ahead and placing QR codes throughout your library and city, develop a plan and strategy for your QR code campaign. Below are some best practices to help you get started:

Set Goals

Think about what you want to achieve by implementing a QR code campaign. Do you want people to be aware of specific resources your library has? Do you want patrons to be able to quickly access recommended reading lists? Or are you just trying to be trendy? Setting goals will help you to keep on track in your QR code endeavor.

Plan Your Technology

Decide which software application you will use to create, maintain, store, and track your QR codes. Waters (2012) suggests that the tool you use to create QR codes should accommodate four common data types: URL, plain text, phone, and short message service (SMS).

Decide who will be creating the codes, one person or a team.

Determine whether naming conventions are needed (Murphy 2012).

Select Your Content

Select the content or resources you want to promote and ensure it is accessible using a mobile device. Keep in mind that QR codes may point to content that is not optimized on a mobile phone (Pulliam and Landry 2011). You may need to reformat content so it displays correctly on mobile devices, or decide to not use QR codes that point to nonmobile-friendly content.

Relevance is an important component of content selection. QR codes should point to content or resources that are relevant to patrons (Elmore and Stephens 2012), as opposed to using the technology as a trendy marketing campaign.

Know Your Patrons

Consider your patron base and be aware that not all patrons know what QR codes are, know what they are used for, or even have the technology to use them.

You may need to adjust your campaign, provide additional instructions with the code, or offer brief classes on the technology.

Below are examples of QR code projects that had low usage, possibly because librarian expectations on how patrons would use QR codes did not match patron mental models.

Walsh (2010) states that a low percentage of students and staff from British colleges knew what QR codes were. For those who were aware of QR codes, finding and installing the appropriate reader was somewhat challenging.

Robinson (2010) had a similar finding to Walsh and noted that with regard to QR reader applications for users, "There needs to be a good reason for users to take the trouble to load and use them" (83).

Chesterfield County Public Library may have overestimated the number of teens who owned smartphones in their 2011 scavenger hunt and suggested that some teens may not have wanted to bother downloading and installing a QR code reader application (Cerny and Holcomb 2012).

Dobbs (2011) mentions the need to explain to middle school faculty and students what QR codes are.

Train Your Staff

Staff training will help create a successful campaign. Your staff will have varying degrees of technological knowledge; some may not be familiar with using mobile devices, while others will be able to help with the training.

It is important to train staff on how to turn on devices and install QR reader applications, as well as how and why to scan QR codes.

Test Your Codes

Testing is extremely important. Test your QR codes with different mobile devices and readers. Make sure the code is working the way you intend.

Consider having several staff members help with testing. By including staff in the testing phase, you can capitalize on training staff about the library's QR code project and have an array of different devices test the QR code.

Market Your Codes

Market your QR code campaign inside and outside of your library.

Murphy (2012) recommends posting QR codes as you would an art display and also in unexpected areas. Print them on posters, signs, and brochures. Embed them in e-mail signatures, on social networks, on Web pages, and anywhere else you would normally post information about library events and resources.

Offer Support

Not all patrons know how to use QR codes or how to download and install a QR reader application. Support may include signs near the code explaining how to find and install a QR code reader (Elmore and Stephens 2012).

Provide the URL

Some people may not be able to scan the QR code due to technical difficulties or they may not use a device capable of scanning QR codes. Always include a URL—preferably a short URL—so patrons have an alternative way to access the content you are providing.

▓ CASE STUDIES ▓

Libraries are using QR codes in a variety of ways. The examples below demonstrate how libraries are using QR codes and how patrons have responded to the technology.

QR Codes for Promotion of Library Resources and Events

Pulliam and Landry (2011) discuss very low patron use of QR codes used to promote Banned Books week in 2009 at Providence College Library. The library later created a QR code display used to promote resources and mobile services, which received more use than their initial endeavor.

At the University of Huddersfield, Walsh (2010) describes several ways in which QR codes are used in the library. An effort to raise awareness of electronic resources such as e-books and journals was made by putting QR codes on the shelf next to physical copies. Walsh reports low usage of QR codes with this service.

University of Fairbanks Rasmuson Library used QR codes to advertise a library survey. QR codes were printed onto table tents and distributed throughout the library and on campus. Out of 207 respondents, 66 accessed the survey by scanning the QR codes (personal knowledge from author Ilana Kingsley).

California's Contra Costa County Library (CCCL), winner of several awards for their Snap & Go campaign, uses QR codes inside and outside of the library to promote resources. Target audiences of the campaign are public transit users and people who are unable to physically visit their community library (MacKinnon and Sanford 2010). CCCL reported a 16 percent increase in usage of their mobile website after launching the campaign (Sanford 2012).

Florida's Broward County Libraries (BCL), in partnership with the Broward County Transit Central Terminal, has posted metal signs in the transit center. The signs, which have QR codes that link to e-books and to the BCL WoW mobile app, enable commuters to access library resources remotely (McElrath 2012).

FIGURE 9.4
QR code campaign for e-books, King County (WA) Library System

Washington's King County Libraries (KCL) began a successful QR advertising campaign in the Seattle/Tacoma airport as part of their Take Time to Read promotion. Elsa Steele reported (in personal communication with author Ilana Kingsley) that a full-size advertisement containing a QR code linking to their electronic book download page was located in a busy concourse area of the airport and received 1,196 scans in a three-month period. The advertisement is shown in figure 9.4.

Incentives to Use QR Codes

The University of Bath Library promoted the use of QR codes within the library by offering chocolate to students who scanned a QR code in the library catalog (Elmore and Stephens 2012). According to Elmore and Stephens, 360 chocolates were handed out, thus "possibly suggesting that the scheme provided a useful stepping stone to further use of QR codes" (2012, 33).

QR Codes for Library Instruction

In an effort to highlight point-of-need library instruction, the University of Huddersfield Library (Walsh 2010) developed a pilot project using QR codes to link patrons to instructional videos. Similar to the library's effort to raise awareness of electronic resources, QR codes were placed in the physical world, either on the shelf or next to a machine (e.g., printer). The author reported low usage with this service.

Loughborough University developed a pilot QR code program where QR codes were printed on posters and brochures linked to instructional PDF handouts. Results showed some use of the QR codes, although less than expected. Students scanned codes only if the linked information was relevant to their needs (Elmore and Stephens 2012). The authors tracked the location of scans to outside of the library, which means that students took a brochure and later scanned the code.

QR Codes for Scavenger Hunts

Wells (2012) noted that a scavenger hunt for Conservatory of Music students at the University of the Pacific was used as instructional tool to introduce students to the music collection. Students' evaluation of the activity was positive.

Chesterfield County Public Library created iHunt and mini-iHunt, which were QR code scavenger hunts to promote library services and resources to teens. Cerny and Holcomb (2012) concluded that the most challenging part of the scavenger hunt was finding participants.

QR Codes in Library Catalog Records

The University of Bath Library, an early adopter of QR codes, began embedding QR codes to records in their library catalog in 2009. QR codes were displayed only if the item was physically available on the shelf. Robinson (2010) found that a smaller number of users than originally envisioned actually scanned QR codes in the library catalog.

■ ■ ■

CONCLUSIONS

The use of QR codes in libraries has come a long way in a short time. Libraries are using QR codes in a variety of creative ways. QR codes are a no- to low-cost technology and are easy to create, place, and track. When starting a QR code campaign, it is important to remember some of the limitations of QR codes and to provide alternative means of access for these patrons. These limitations include:

- Not all patrons own a smartphone or mobile device that can read QR codes.
- Patrons owning devices that can read QR codes may not know what the codes are.
- Patrons may not want to take the time to download QR codes reader applications.

In spite of these limitations, some libraries have found QR codes to be an effective way to promote library resources both in and outside of the library. Libraries who have had success with QR codes have heavily advertised the codes outside of the library. With a little advanced planning, you and your library can launch a successful QR code campaign. As smartphone use increases, it is likely library patrons will find additional value in QR codes.

REFERENCES

Ashford, Robin. 2010. "QR Codes and Academic Libraries." *College & Research Libraries News* 71 (10): 526–530.

Cerny, Jessica, and JoLynn Holcomb. 2012. "Using a QR Code Scavenger Hunt (iHunt) to Promote Library Services to Teens." *Virginia Libraries* 58 (1): 39–42.

Denso. 2001. "QR Code and Two-Dimensional Code Scanners." Last updated 2001. www.globaldenso.com/TECHNOLOGY/tec-report/2001/pdf/T2001_S39.pdf.

Dobbs, Cheri. 2011. "QR Codes in the Library: "It's Not Your Mother's Barcode!" *Library Media Connection* 30 (1): 14–16.

Elmore, Lauren, and Derek Stephens. 2012. "The Application of QR Codes in UK Academic Libraries." *New Review of Academic Librarianship* 18 (1): 26–42.

MacKinnon, Paula, and Cathy Sanford. 2010. "Snap & Go: A QReative Case in Point." *Library Hi Tech News* 27 (4): 5–8.

McElrath, Catherine. 2012. "Books and Buses: Libraries and Transit Bring Free Downloadable Books to the Central Bus Terminal in Downtown Fort Lauderdale."

Broward County (FL) press release. March 30. http://webapps.broward.org/newsrelease/AdminDisplayMessages.aspx?intMessageId=3667.

Murphy, J. 2012. *Location-Aware Services and QR Codes for Libraries*. Chicago: ALA TechSource.

Pulliam, Beatrice and Chris Landry. 2011. "Tag, You're It! Using QR Codes to Promote Library Services." *Reference Librarian* 52 (1): 68–74.

Robinson, K. 2010. "QR Codes and Their Applications for Libraries: A Case Study from the University of Bath Library." In *M-libraries 2: A Virtual Library in Everyone's Pocket*, edited by M. Ally and G. Needham, 81–83. London: Facet Publishing.

Rouillard, J. 2008. "Contextual QR Codes." *Third International Multi-Conference on Computing in the Global Information Technology*, 50–55.

Sanford, Cathy. 2012. "Contra Costa County Library Wins 2012 John Cotton Dana Public Relations Award." Contra Costa County (CA) Library press release. April 24. http://ccclib.org/press_releases/johncottondana2012.html.

Sekyere, Kwabena. 2012. "QR Codes in Libraries: Uses and Usage Tracking." *College & Undergraduate Libraries* 19 (1): 95–100.

Walsh, Andrew. 2010. "QR Codes: Using Mobile Phones to Deliver Library Instruction and Help at the Point of Need." *Journal of Information Literacy* 4 (1): 55–63.

Waters, Joe. 2012. *QR Codes for Dummies Portable Edition*. New York: For Dummies.

Wells, Veronica A. 2012. "Hunting for QR Codes: Linking Students to the Music Collection." *Music Reference Services Quarterly* 15 (3): 137–148.

Whitchurch, Michael J. 2012. "A Quick Response: QR Code use at the Harold B. Lee Library." *Reference Librarian* 53 (4): 392–402.

Winter, Mick. 2011. *Scan Me: Everybody's Guide to the Magical World of QR Codes—Barcodes, Mobile Devices and Hyperlinking the Real to the Virtual*. Napa, CA: Westsong Publications.

Twitter as a Marketing Tool for Libraries

Laura Carscaddon, Georgia State University

Kimberly Chapman, University of Arizona

WHY TWITTER?

Twitter is a microblogging service that allows users to post messages, called tweets, of up to 140 characters and to broadcast these messages immediately to the web. According to the Pew Research Center, 15 percent of online adults use Twitter, with 8 percent making use of it on a typical day (Smith and Brenner 2012). The same report showed higher Twitter use among certain demographic groups, particularly African Americans with 28 percent and young adults with 31 percent of the 18-to-24 age group using Twitter (Smith and Brenner 2012). Twitter is one of the easiest ways to start testing the social media waters. No specialized tools are required to use Twitter, and with more than 140 million active users, there is a very good chance that at least some people in your community are using Twitter (Twitter 2012c).

Libraries are using Twitter for a variety of communication purposes. Some libraries use it to listen to what their customers are saying about the library. Bell states that Twitter is a "golden opportunity to connect with members of the library community" (2012, p. 218). Some libraries use Twitter to make connections to people and organizations within their communities (Gunton and Davis 2012). Other libraries use Twitter to promote their library programs and services, as well as relevant items from other organizations. Twitter can be an excellent way to learn what your customers are thinking, to build conversations with your users, to address customer concerns, and to advocate for your programs and services.

This chapter provides information on implementing and maintaining a Twitter account, offers best practices, and suggests tips and tricks for a successful Twitter marketing campaign. Examples of libraries "doing it well" are included.

ESTABLISHING A TWITTER ACCOUNT

Start your Twitter experience by going to www.twitter.com to set up your account. You will need an e-mail address, a strong password, a user name, and an icon to associate with your account. Use a general e-mail account from your library rather than an e-mail account associated with a specific person within the library. If you do not already have a general e-mail account for the library, use a free e-mail service (such as Google Gmail) to set one up.

User Name

Think carefully about the user name you select because this will be how your library is known on Twitter and the name people will use when mentioning your library on Twitter. Keep the user name short and recognizable: short, because every character in your user name is one less character available for the content of a tweet that mentions your library, and recognizable so that that your Twitter account is clearly linked to your library brand (Lacy 2011). Shown below are examples of short and recognizable Twitter account names:

- @NYPL: New York Public Library
- @Provlib: Providence (RI) Public Library
- @gsu_library: Georgia State University Library
- @pimalibrary: Pima County Public Library

    This system has additional accounts for each branch, such as:

    @MainLib
    @NaniniLib
    @WoodsLib

If your library has multiple branches, you can choose to use naming conventions similar to the Pima County Public Library's if the programs and services offered at each branch are distinct. However, remember that it will be more work to keep each account updated regularly. Provide your full library name as the real name for your

Twitter account. People can search for your library's name if they don't know the library's user name, so this gives them one more way to find your library on Twitter.

Icon and Profile

The next step is to customize your Twitter profile, as shown in figure 10.1. Libraries should make the most of their social media presence by adding images and photos. Be sure to include the logo for your library. Using images and logos, as well as the same colors as your website, will help brand your Twitter account as being a part of your library. Most people are visual; the use of existing logos and colors allows them to easily recognize your social media outlets. If you do not have or cannot use your library logo, use a picture of your library or your staff. Whatever picture is used, it needs to be specific to your library, not just a generic library image.

A short biography is helpful, although if you have associated your full library name with your account, it is not absolutely necessary. With your account

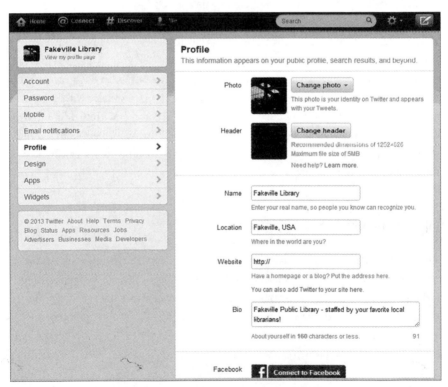

FIGURE 10.1
Creating a Twitter profile

established, you can now link it to your library's other social media accounts, such as Facebook, as well as to a social media management suite. Social media management suites are discussed later in this chapter.

Some accounts have a blue check mark next to their name, such as @Library-Journal. That is an indication that Twitter has taken extra steps to ensure that the account is actually associated with a specific person or organization. When verifying accounts, Twitter focuses on "highly sought users in music, acting, fashion, government, politics, religion, journalism, media, advertising, business, and other key interest areas. We verify business partners from time to time and individuals at high risk of impersonation" (Twitter 2012b). Very few libraries operate as verified accounts; those that do tend to be government agencies, such as the Library of Congress. Verified accounts cannot be requested. If Twitter decides that your account needs verification they will take the steps to do so. Because most accounts on Twitter are not verified, do not be concerned if your library account is not.

In your account settings, there is an option to "Protect My Tweets" (Twitter 2012b). The idea of protecting your tweets may sound like something good to do; however, in reality, it is not a good strategy for a library's Twitter account. What Twitter means by the term "protecting" is marking every tweet you send as private, so only those followers you have approved can see your tweets. While this is useful for individuals who use Twitter to communicate with each other, your Twitter objectives are probably to communicate and engage openly with your user community. Keep the tweets public. Libraries want to connect with their communities, share information, and promote programs, and thus want people to see their information. Protect your Twitter account's integrity in other ways through such things as establishing strong passwords and limiting account access (Twitter 2012a).

DEVELOPING A TWITTER PLAN

Although creating a Twitter account is easy, as shown above, it is important to remember that the essence of social media tools is that they are maintained regularly and remain engaging to users. Twitter is no exception—a library's presence should be maintained just as other public service points are maintained.

Libraries need to spend time planning their approach to Twitter (Bell 2012; Jennings 2012). Think about your customers' viewpoints and what you want them to experience if they follow you on Twitter or read your library's tweets. Establishing objectives helps you decide what to tweet and how often. In addition, having a plan in place helps you evaluate the success of your Twitter efforts.

Begin the planning process with some background research. This gives you a sense of how your customers are using Twitter and how other libraries are using it. First, "listen" to Twitter to find out if your community talks about the library already. A simple way to do this is to search your library's name using the "Search Twitter" feature located at https://twitter.com/search. Are people talking about your library, and if so, what are they saying? It is good practice to incorporate regular listening into your overall Twitter strategy. (Searching Twitter is covered in more detail later in this chapter.) Take time also to identify libraries similar to yours that have a Twitter presence, particularly if there are other libraries that your organization uses as models or peers. Evaluate their Twitter presence in terms of both the frequency of tweets and the content that is tweeted in order to gather ideas on how your library might use Twitter.

After the background work is completed, think about how you will use Twitter. Are you going to use it to connect with other organizations? Are you planning to promote your programs and services? Regardless of the intent, it is important to recognize that by establishing a public Twitter presence for your library, you are creating a virtual service point. Customers will expect to interact with you and receive responses; thus you will need to address how your library will manage those interactions in a timely fashion.

If your library already has a social media strategy consider how to incorporate Twitter into the strategy. For example, how will your tweets differ from Facebook posts? What will you post, and how often? If Twitter is the start of your library's social media efforts, think about how and where the information you post to Twitter will come from. For instance, does your library already have regular programs and events for you to tweet about?

You will also need to think about who is going to tweet on behalf of your library: is this one person's duty or will there be a group of tweeters? If there are multiple people participating, make sure that you have agreed-upon processes to manage who is doing what and when. While it is a great start to have one enthusiastic person to manage Twitter regularly and who can lead the library into the Twittersphere, you can also create buy-in and support in the library by having additional people involved. This will also help with continuity of service when people are out sick, on vacation, or on personal leave; therefore, considering how your library will sustain its Twitter presence in both the short and the long term is an important part of the planning process.

FINDING, FOLLOWING, AND TWEETING

Now that your account is established and a plan is created, you can start following people and organizations, and start sending out your own tweets. The first step is to find others to follow. During the account setup process, Twitter prompts you to choose ten people or organizations to follow. You can start or stop following others on Twitter at any time. In order to find more people or organizations to follow after the setup process, enter names of people, organizations, or topics in the Twitter search box (fig. 10.2).

Public libraries may find it useful to follow local organizations, leaders, and select businesses in their community. For example, the Pima County (AZ) Public Library has chosen to follow a wide variety of people and organizations both local and national (fig. 10.3). Clicking on the followers list for their main account (@pimalibrary) on October 26, 2012, showed that they were following approximately 1,700 people, including:

FIGURE 10.2
Twitter search for *libraries*

- @SeisCurbside, a local food truck
- @EllerCollege, the business school at the local university
- @IdeaFunding, a local entrepreneurship center
- @TucsonArtInformation, local art information in Tuscon, Arizona

In addition to serving as an example of a "following page," the Pima County Public Library is a good model to follow when customizing your Twitter account with a different look and feel. You can choose from premade themes or add your own colors and design customizations. To customize your Twitter screen presence, click on the "Settings" button (the gear icon), choose "Edit Profile," and go to the "Design" section. As with all social media tools, it is best to connect marketing efforts to the library using the same logo, colors, and naming conventions.

Academic libraries should follow local organizations as well, but it is best to first look for offices, colleges, and departments on their campus, student groups, as well as other related entities. Following stakeholders and current or potential user groups is a good way to keep up with what is happening on campus and in the community. Using this information, your library can look for ways to tie into activities and events. If the other campus units are active tweeters, you may also be able to develop useful new connections to share information.

153

FIGURE 10.3
Following on Twitter, Pima County (AZ) Public Library

It is often best to start following a small number of people initially in order to keep up with reading, and using, their tweets. You do not have to follow everyone who follows you. Read some of their tweets and decide if they will be useful to follow. Also keep in mind that new followers may be spammers or bots that automatically follow new accounts.

You can start tweeting at any time by clicking within the "Compose New Tweet" box on your Twitter homepage. Click on the "Home" button on any Twitter screen to return to this screen. Decide what to tweet. If you approached Twitter by determining the purpose of your Twitter account as was recommended earlier, you can now implement your strategies. Depending on how you have decided to use your Twitter account, you might tweet about:

- Events and programs
- New books
- Pictures of your staff and your library
- Unique or fun things that your library has to offer. For example, the Fairfield (CT) Public Library (@fairfieldpublib) had life-size cardboard figures made of some of their librarians and staff. The library's webmaster, Merry Uk, set up a Twitter account for the cutout of her with the account @CardboardMerry. While not an officially sanctioned library account, CardboardMerry did promote the library through her tweets.
- Reply to comments people make about your library
- Interesting links (see the bitly section of this article for more information on strategies for handling links)

After you click in the "Compose New Tweet" field, Twitter counts how many characters you have typed so you know how many you have left to work with. In addition, you have options for adding a photo and for adding a location. You can also edit your location in your profile so that tweets from your library are always indicated with the location. If you are tweeting directly to another person or organization, be sure to include their user name with the @ symbol so that that they will receive your tweets. You can also tweet them directly on their Twitter page.

Listening to Twitter

One of the most useful ways to use Twitter is to search it regularly to find out how people are talking about your library. The most direct way people mention your library on Twitter is by using your user name; for example, @fakevillelib. These mentions are easily found as part of the "Connect" function on your Twitter page. Other people may not know your user name or may not bother with finding it. You can still find and respond to what they are saying if you choose to.

Twitter has a good search function built in that lets you easily save searches. Any searches that you save on the Twitter site will automatically bring results into a social media management suite if you use one. You can also set up really simple syndication (RSS) feeds into a reader for search results. Saving searches, such as the ones below, can help you find a good portion of what others are saying about your library. You may not find everything, and if your library name is similar to others, you might bring in some false results; however, it is still more helpful to search regularly than not to know what your patrons are writing. You can always change your saved searches to be more precise. Suggested searches include:

- "[Full library name]"
- [City name] "public library"
- "[University name] library"
- "[Short form of university name] library"
- Any of the above with the word problem included
- University abbreviation and problem, or the nickname for problems at the school, such as

    TUproblems (Temple University)
    BigOrangeScrew (University of Tennessee, Knoxville)

- Use Twitter's advanced search with any of the above to include tweets that may be positive or negative, indicated by the :) or :(emoticons. Also search for a question mark, which may indicate a potential issue or reference question.

For more information on searching, operators, and access to the advanced search screen, see https://twitter.com/search.

Twitter Vocabulary

Similar to the development of any social media—and in general, any new technology—Twitter has some unique terminology. Common verbage includes:

tweet: a message of up to 140 characters posted on Twitter

Twitter stream: a series of tweets from a Twitter account

retweet (RT): a tweet forwarded by someone to his followers

follower: an individual or organization who chooses to follow your Twitter account and receive all your tweets

following: individuals or organizations that you have chosen to follow on your Twitter account; you will receive their tweets

mention: using *@username* to talk to or mention a specific Twitter account in a tweet

hashtag: a word or phrase preceded by # used as a tag. Clicking on a hashtag will search for all public instances of its use; hashtags can also be included in saved searches.

Hashtags

In a very broad sense, hashtags are the subject headings of Twitter. There are no standards or authority control behind hashtags. Anything can be a hashtag—all you have to do is precede a word or phrase with the # symbol. If you use a phrase, make sure not to include spaces. For example: use *#librariesareamazing*, not *#librar ies are amazing*.

If you have recently attended a conference, you may have seen a statement mentioning the "official" hashtag for the event. With this hashtag, people at the conference and others who may be interested know how to search in order to find Tweets coming from the conference and are able to join in the conversation. There is no official governing body that designates hashtags; hashtags are declared as official by the organizer of the event. For example, the 2013 ALA Midwinter Meeting has the official hashtag *#alamw13*.

Hashtags can be used for other reasons. If you have a standing acronym for you library—for instance, DCPL or NYPL—use it in your tweets and as a search term. Participate in Twitter using established hashtags as well. There is a long-running hashtag of *#fridayreads* where people put out what they are reading on a given Friday. There is also the *#ff* hashtag, which stands for "follow Friday." Use this and mention some of the accounts that you follow along with their @username. These can result in a follow back, or at least a thanks from them, and can be a way to promote goodwill among Tweeters in your community. Finally, remember that hashtags can also be humorous, sarcastic, or anything in between. For example, someone might tweet, "I'm so excited to return these library books! #payingfinesyay!"

Tweeting Your Library

You have 140 characters per tweet to share information. While there are services that allow you to write a longer tweet that is linked to one posted on Twitter, this is not a recommended technique. Your followers aren't getting the short, simple information they want. If you include a link that is buried under a link to a longer tweet, followers will need to click twice to get to what you want them to see, and you will lose people before that second link because this is not a usual Twitter practice. These links may also be difficult for people using Twitter via mobile devices.

If you are tweeting about events or programs and people can opt to link to a webpage for more information, consider using bitly links within your tweets. bitly (https://bitly.com/) is a free service that you can use to "organize your links, count your clicks, and share your links across Facebook, Twitter, and email," as described on their site. For example, compare and contrast the two links below:

- www.fakevillelibrary.org/eventsandprograms/
- http://bit.ly/Y9WwZv

Twitter will automatically shorten lengthy URLs with bitly when you type them into a tweet; however, you can also set up a bitly account and shorten the URLs yourself. The advantage of using bitly URLs is that you can use the website to track how many people click on the links that you broadcast.

Now that you are tweeting about the library, let others know that your library tweets. Make sure that all library staff know about the library's new Twitter presence. Promote your account on the website. Add icons and "Follow" buttons to your library's website to make it easy for people to find and follow your account. Choose among several functions for buttons or between two different styles from those provided by Twitter (fig. 10.4). Twitter also provides information about using their logo at https://twitter.com/logo.

In addition to adding Twitter buttons to your library website, you can embed your Twitter stream directly into your website. Embedding your Twitter stream lets people easily see your tweets even if they do not have an account. It also provides a link to your account so that they can easily follow you if they are Twitter users themselves. To embed your Twitter stream on your library website, go to https://twitter.com/settings/widgets. Click "Create New" to get the code for a widget that you can embed, and then copy and paste the code into your website.

A good example of a Twitter widget on a web page is shown in figure 10.5. This example is from the American Library Association's Midwinter Meeting 2013

FIGURE 10.4
Twitter buttons

FIGURE 10.5
Twitter widget embedded on the ALA Midwinter Meeting website

webpage, http://alamw13.ala.org/. The Twitter stream has been labeled "Midwinter Buzz" and updates in real time. Notice the social media buttons on the left below the Twitter stream that indicate how people can connect with the event.

In addition to including buttons on your website and embedding your Twitter stream into appropriate library webpages, you can tie your Twitter account to other social media accounts. If your library has a Facebook account, you can link the two accounts so that your tweets are automatically posted to Facebook, thus letting you connect with users there as well. From your Twitter profile page, scroll down, click the "Connect to Facebook" button, and authorize access. Your tweets will now automatically post to your library's Facebook account.

SOCIAL MEDIA MANAGEMENT SYSTEMS

If you choose, there are social media management tools for maintaining one or more social media accounts. Two of the most used are TweetDeck and HootSuite. Both of these allow you to:

- Send tweets immediately
- Schedule tweets for later posting; this is handy for planned advertising of events, contests, and other organized activities
- Monitor your saved searches
- Track direct messages and mentions of your library
- Post pictures and links to your followers
- Post to Facebook and Twitter from the same site

TweetDeck (https://twitter.com/TweetDeck) offers a browser-based version, a Chrome app, and a download, while HootSuite (https://hootsuite.com/) is browser-based only. Both TweetDeck and HootSuite have mobile apps available for iOS and Android devices. Apps are useful options if you want to tweet directly to your followers from library events.

Both tools require you to set up a separate account and then link your Twitter account. If you use one of these tools, be sure to use a different password from your Twitter account. That way, if multiple people are tweeting from your library's Twitter account, you can give them the TweetDeck or HootSuite password but not the one to your Twitter account.

TweetDeck has been part of Twitter since December 2011 and is free to use. As new features roll out to Twitter, they are more likely to arrive at TweetDeck in a timely manner. TweetDeck allows you to link and update the library's Facebook page from that account.

HootSuite, on the other hand, is a separate company and has both free and paid levels of service. At the free level, you can add up to five profiles from social networks, including Twitter, Facebook, LinkedIn, Foursquare, and more. Hoot-Suite also allows you to add an unlimited number of HootSuite apps to increase your connections; thus, additional accounts, such as Tumblr, Flickr, or Youtube accounts, can be included as well. If your library has an RSS feed for a blog or for new book lists, you can add two feeds with a free account and automatically send a tweet with those. The free HootSuite account also provides some basic analytics for your social media accounts by pulling information from other services, such as Google Analytics, into a report.

The paid level of HootSuite allows you to have a team who can post to your account—which is useful if you have multiple people among your library's staff who tweet, as they can all have access from within HootSuite. One additional user comes with the paid account, and each additional user will cost more. Paid accounts also provide a more detailed analytics report to subscribers.

You do not have to use either of these to get started using Twitter, but using a social media management tool can make it simpler to respond to your users efficiently. In addition, the analytics tools offered may be useful as you evaluate your Twitter presence.

EVALUATING, ASSESSING, AND USING STATISTICS

Libraries should evaluate and assess their Twitter presence just as they evaluate and assess other social media presences. Also consider assessing your Twitter presence as you do other service points, such as the reference desk or virtual reference services. Relate the evaluation to the objectives that were established in the Twitter plan. Determine the best way to evaluate the objectives.

Simply counting the number of followers for your Twitter account is not necessarily useful, as the number will have no context. What is the number being compared to? What does it mean? In addition, you may have people who read your tweets but do not choose to follow the library. While it may be useful to track how many followers the library has over time, it is important to think about what that number does or does not mean. It may also be interesting to your library to look at who is following your Twitter account. Are they library customers, other organizations in your community, or other libraries?

If you use bitly links to lead users to your website, promotional materials, and so on, you can track the number of people who read your tweets and clicked through for further information. This will give you some additional insight about your users' areas of interest and you can customize future tweets accordingly.

"Listening" to Twitter is a strategy recommended earlier in this chapter. Plan to periodically analyze mentions of your library on Twitter, noting positive, negative, and neutral comments (Doshi 2012). If your library currently has a plan for evaluating customer comments, such as a library feedback form or comment cards, evaluating Twitter comments could be incorporated into existing work.

Because customers will interact with you via Twitter and expect you to respond, you can incorporate your Twitter assessment into whatever method you use for tracking customer inquiries via other channels. For instance, report reference transactions or other inquiries that were initiated via Twitter. Additionally, Twitter should be incorporated into other library evaluation processes, such as by including "Twitter" as an option on program evaluation forms that are used at library programs and events.

In addition to assessing use of your Twitter account by customers, also evaluate the time staff spend participating in Twitter so that everyone understands the level of support needed to maintain this social media presence. While monitoring Twitter and posting tweets may take only a few minutes of someone's time each day, it is work that should be recognized by library management.

The above assessment methods may provide you with enough information to keep your library informed about the success of your library's Twitter account. In addition, there are a variety of tools to evaluate various social media applications, and of course, tools are constantly changing and evolving. Twitter itself has discussed beta analytics tools, but these are still in development. Although many of the tools are oriented to support marketing strategies for businesses, libraries can take advantage of these tools too. Consider experimenting with free analysis tools that can help you visualize data (Bea 2013). These tools include Twitonomy (www.twitonomy.com), which tracks Twitter conversations and shows how you have been using Twitter. Twitter Counter (www.twittercounter.com) can be used to count numbers and compare your account against another account, such as those libraries you identified in your background research.

BEST PRACTICES AND CONCLUSIONS

After your Twitter account is established and operating, there are some additional things to keep in mind in order to keep your account useful to both your library's followers and anyone who discovers your library's Tweets:

Best Practices: Tweet Security

- Maintain strong passwords. The library's Twitter account does represent the library, and you do not want a password that could be easily guessed.
- If someone with access to the library's Twitter account leaves the library, ensure that the password is changed.
- Do not click on links in direct messages if you do not know where the link goes. This is one of the most common ways that Twitter accounts are hacked.

Best Practices: Tweets and Content

- Create a plan for Twitter use and reevaluate it periodically.
- Stay active with the account—keep tweeting information for your followers to read.
- Set aside a few minutes every workday to listen for mentions of your library and find replies to your tweets.
- Keep your library staff informed and excited about Twitter, as some of the best content ideas may come from other library staff.
- Let your library's personality shine through your tweets.

Twitter provides your library with new opportunities to connect with your library users in meaningful ways. You can share information, build community, start conversations, and listen to your users using a service that is free and available to anyone with an Internet connection. Twitter works well on its own or as part of a comprehensive social media and promotions strategy. Remember to develop an effective social media management plan. Join other libraries using Twitter and start tweeting!

REFERENCES

Bea, Francis. 2013. "Our Favorite, Free Twitter Analytics Services for Casual and Professional Users." Digital Trends. January 26. www.digitaltrends.com/social-media/top-five-twitter-analytics/.

Bell, Stephen. 2012. "Students Tweet the Darndest Things about Your Library—and Why You Need to Listen." *Reference Services Review* 40 (2): 217–220.

Doshi, Ameet. 2012. "Just the Right Tweet at the Right Time." *Reference Services Review* 40 (2): 221–223.

Lacy, K. 2011. *Twitter Marketing For Dummies*. New Jersey: John Wiley & Sons.

Jennings, S. 2012. "To Tweet, Or Not To Tweet." *Reference Services Review* 40 (2): 214–216.

Gunton, Lyndelle, and Kate Davis. 2012. "Beyond Broadcasting: Customer Service, Community and Information Experience in the Twittersphere." *Reference Services Review* 40 (2): 224–227.

Smith, A. D., and J Brenner. 2012. "Twitter Use 2012." May 31. Pew Internet & American Life Project. www.pewinternet.org/~/media//Files/Reports/2012/PIP_Twitter_Use_2012.pdf.

Twitter. 2012a. "About Public and Protected Tweets." Last updated 2013. https://support.twitter.com/articles/14016.

Twitter. 2012b. "FAQs about Verified Accounts." Last updated 2013. https://support.twitter.com/groups/31-twitter-basics/topics/111-features/articles/119135-faqs-about-verified-accounts.

Twitter. 2012c. "Twitter Turns Six." Twitter blog. March 21. https://blog.twitter.com/2012/twitter-turns-six.

About the Editor and Contributors

EDITOR

BETH THOMSETT-SCOTT is currently the engineering librarian at the University of North Texas Libraries. In her previous role as Reference Unit manager, she assisted with establishing the libraries' Meebo service, as well as their chat and text messaging services. Thomsett-Scott has been with the UNT Libraries for ten years, with previous positions held at the University of Guelph and University of Western Ontario Libraries. She holds a a bachelor of science, a master of science, and a master of library science from the Universities of Guelph, Manitoba, and Western Ontario respectively. Her professional associations include the American Library Association, Special Library Association, and the Texas Library Association, where she has served in various positions. Thomsett-Scott has published in a variety of journals and presented conference sessions in the areas of website usability, mentoring and training reference staff and students, and technology. Her passions include virtual reference, website usability, user satisfaction studies, and technologies for reference, instruction, and liaison.

CONTRIBUTORS

LAURA CARSCADDON is the coordinator of Library Services for Social Sciences, Business, & Education at Georgia State University. She is a graduate of the University of Tennessee School of Information Science. Her research interests include the use of social media in academic libraries as well as strategic plans of ARL libraries.

KIMBERLY CHAPMAN is the Campus Repository Service manager at the University of Arizona Libraries. She is a graduate of the University of Texas at Austin. Her research interests include the use of social media in academic libraries, use of social media to expose and promote digital collections, and library support of scholarly publishing initiatives from journal hosting to institutional repositories.

ANITA R. DRYDEN received her MLS from the University of Pittsburgh in 2009. Currently, she serves as the Systems and Emerging Technologies Librarian at the Briddle Law Library, University of Pennsylvania. Prior to her library career she worked in the marketing industry, and she served on the University of Houston's Marketing Committee in her previous position. Dryden has a strong interest in evidence-based practices, and has spoken regionally and nationally on assessing technology in libraries and research data management. Named as an ALA Emerging Leader in 2012, she continues to be actively involved in LITA and other technology-focused organizations.

KATIE BUEHNER is the coordinator of the Music Library and assistant librarian for Music, Theatre, and Dance at the University of Houston. She holds a master of library science and a master of music in musicology, both from the University of North Texas. She has produced more than one hundred videos for the University of Houston Libraries, including instructional videos, marketing segments, and mashups that highlight the libraries' collections. Her research interests include the library as producer of culture and twentieth-century American opera. Buehner also serves as a lecturer for the Moores School of Music at the University of Houston.

MEMO CORDOVA is an associate professor and librarian at Boise State University's Albertsons Library. He received his MLIS in 2003 from the University of Washington's iSchool. His research interests include the intersection of web applications and technology in education, libraries, and day-to-day life. Cordova teaches a one-credit library research course, is involved in THATCamp events, and liaises with the Anthropology, Psychology, Modern Languages & Literatures, Bilingual Education, and Philosophy departments on campus.

JANET HACK is currently the Research and Instruction Librarian for Science and Online Technologies at the Hoover Library, McDaniel College. She serves as liaison to all the science departments and manages the library's website and other online user interfaces. Janet was formerly Web Services Librarian at the University of

Maryland, Baltimore County (UMBC), where she was responsible for the library's overall web presence. She has a master of library science degree from the University of Maryland, College Park. Her interests include user-centered design, emerging technologies, and distance education.

ILANA KINGSLEY is an associate professor and web librarian at the University of Alaska Fairbanks. Her background is in web development and information architecture. She holds a master's degree in library science and is currently enrolled in a master of education program in online design and innovation.

MEGAN KOCHER is a science librarian at the University of Minnesota Libraries, where she serves as liaison to the Department of Animal Science, the Department of Food Science and Nutrition, and the Department of Soil, Water and Climate. She also curates the Doris S. Kirschner Cookbook Collection and blogs about it at http://z.umn.edu/kirschner. Kocher is interested in technology and communications in libraries and has presented on such topics as QR codes, Moodle as an assessment tool, Google+, and Scrivener.

SHAE MARTINEZ is a librarian at the Texas Health Presbyterian Hospital Dallas, Medical Library. She earned her master's degree in library science from the University of North Texas. Her current interests include social networking in libraries and emerging technologies.

JOYCE McFADDEN works as the Public Services librarian at Baylor Health Sciences Library in Dallas. She spends much of her time supporting nurses and dental students and their research needs, whether within the library or as outreach to the various Baylor Hospital locations. The library has a Facebook account and a Twitter account, and opened a Pinterest account as another avenue to advertise the library's services.

CARRIE MOORE is the head of Information and Research Services and an assistant professor at Albertsons Library, Boise State University. She received her MLS in 2002 from Emporia State University. She focuses on instruction, reference, and outreach services in her position. Her projects range from designing library curriculum that is uniformly taught to every first- and second-year student to working with faculty on new mobile learning initiatives. Moore is currently working with her staff to incorporate mobile devices into library instruction sessions.

167

CAROLYN RAUBER is the Physics, Astronomy, and Earth Sciences librarian at the University of Minnesota, Twin Cities. She received her MLS from the University of Illinois at Urbana-Champaign. She has presented on library gaming programs and scientific data management at national conferences, and is active in the Geoscience Information Society and the Physics, Astronomy, and Mathematics division of the Special Library Association. She is interested in improving customer service and outreach through interactive mediums.

ANNE RAUH is the Engineering and Computer Science librarian for Syracuse University Library. She holds a BA in international studies and an MA in library and information studies, both from the University of Wisconsin–Madison. Rauh is an active member of the American Society for Engineering Education, the Eastern New York Chapter of Association of College and Research Libraries, and Beta Phi Mu. She has presented at conferences throughout the country and has published in the proceedings of the American Society for Engineering Education. Her research interests include citation management tools, library outreach, open access initiatives, and publishing and scholarly communication in science and engineering.

JULIA STRINGFELLOW is an archivist/librarian and assistant professor at Boise State University. She has been in this position since 2010, previously working at Lawrence University and the University of California, Irvine. She received her master of library and information science and her master of arts in history from the University of Wisconsin–Milwaukee in 2002. Stringfellow became a certified archivist in 2010 and is currently the vice president of the Conference of Inter-Mountain Archivists (CIMA). In her current position, she works with the university archives, preserving the records of the university, and also provides instruction sessions for Special Collections and general library instruction. Stringfellow enjoys contributing to the social media platforms supported by the library, including posting to Facebook and Pinterest, and writing posts for the library's blog. Her research interests include local history, university history, and the history of libraries in Idaho.

MINDY TOMLIN is a reference librarian and the outreach coordinator at the Robert R. Muntz Library at the University of Texas at Tyler. Part of her responsibilities as Outreach Coordinator include managing the library's social media accounts, including Facebook. Tomlin has several years of experience in public services in academic, school, and public library settings. Some of her research interests include reference and public services, games in education, information literacy, and Library/Web 2.0. You can find Tomlin online @librarianmindy.

AMY VECCHIONE is the Digital Access librarian and an assistant professor at Albertsons Library, Boise State University. She focuses on emerging technologies, promoting collections, and ensuring digital access to the library in her position. Her projects range from assisting with the instructional design for online course work with information literacy to determining the best resources for a mobile learning program. She is currently working with her staff to develop web apps in support of campus research.

AMY WEST has been the Data Services librarian at the University of Minnesota since 2007, and she was the university's Electronic Government Publications librarian from 1999 to 2007. Over thirteen years of working with government publications and data has left her with an abiding interest in using general purpose tools to help users discover highly specialized content as easily as possible.

Index